DEDICATED
TO THE STRONG MEN
I HAVE KNOWN

SECRETS OF STRENGTH

THE AUTHOR AS HE IS TODAY

SECRETS
OF STRENGTH

By

EARLE LIEDERMAN

America's Leading Director of
Physical Education

Published by

EARLE LIEDERMAN

305 BROADWAY, NEW YORK

PRINTED IN U. S. A.

PREFACE

WHEN you go to the theatre and become absorbed in the play, you seldom give a thought to what is going on behind the scenes. To the public the back stage is somewhat of a mystery. The illusion of the play would undoubtedly be spoiled if the public could look behind the wings.

Like plays, books are presented at their best to the reader, and it is seldom known why and how they came into being. If the reader could see the original manuscript of the book, with all its scribbling, corrections and blots, considerable interest would be lost for the story.

Just as the actor lives his part, so the author must literally breathe with his characters. However, this is not a story book; nevertheless, I have lived and dreamed every one of the hours all over again that I have spent with the various strong men who are mentioned within these pages.

While it took me but a short time to actually write the original manuscript, it took me years of thought and planning to gather all the facts together, once more, in my memory. They were like pleasant day dreams. Some plans were formed while I roamed the interior of Alaska, some in Europe, still others under the lazy sun of the Tropics.

Throughout my travels, I met many Strong Men, and when I did, it was like meeting friends, for you know, one Strong Man is always a friend to the other, even though they have never been introduced. They have been through the same hardships and experienced the same progress in molding their bodies to their maximum development and power. For every Strong Man I met, I met thousands of weaklings. Poor health was evident everywhere and even where health reigned, strength was lacking.

So many times, if it were possible, I have longed to gather all the weak ones, interest them more thoroughly in their bodies and explain to each and every one, how he could, with but little effort, quickly improve his physique and strength. This was impossible. I therefore resolved to tell the world what I know of the word "Strength." My plans increased and my mind seemed filled to the bursting point with material to tell to those weak individuals, and like a talkative woman who has been suppressed in her speech for a while and then suddenly released, the words burst forth in such rapidity, that it took me but a few weeks to write them down. I offer them for your approval in this book and I hope the readers will derive the benefits from these pages that I have aimed to give them.

CONTENTS

CHAPTER   PAGE

      PREFACE   9

      INTRODUCTION   13

    I   INHERITED AND ACQUIRED STRENGTH   23

   II   POWER AND STRENGTH (SIZE AND WEIGHT)   41

  III   STRENGTH THROUGH MUSCULAR DEVELOP-
           MENT   57

   IV   ARE SMALL BONES A BAR TO STRENGTH?   87

    V   STRENGTH THROUGH NATURAL ADVANTAGES   106

   VI   "QUALITY OF MUSCLE THE BASIS OF
           STRENGTH"   116

  VII   "STRENGTH THROUGH SYMMETRY"   131

VIII   STRENGTH FROM PERFECT DIGESTION   142

   IX   THE IMPORTANCE OF BIG LUNGS AND A
           STRONG HEART   149

    X   THE SECRET OF NERVOUS ENERGY   161

   XI   BUILDING VITAL FORCE AND RESERVE
           ENERGY   172

  XII   BUILDING STRENGTH   200

LIST OF ILLUSTRATIONS

The Author as He Is Today . . . . *Frontispiece*

PAGE

Eugen Sandow 27
George Hackenschmidt 33
George Lurich 39
Edward Aston 45
Joseph Nordquest 51
Arthur Saxon 59
Arthur Saxon 65
Thomas Inch 71
Antone Matysek 77
John Y. Smith 83
Louis Cyr 89
Adolph Nordquest 95
Adolph Nordquest 101
Ottley R. Coulter 107
Warren L. Travis 113
George Jowett 119
William Gerardi 125
Tony Massimo 133
Eugen Sandow 139
Eugen Sandow 145
Joseph Nordquest 151
Joseph Nordquest 157
Tony Massimo 163
Joseph Nordquest 169
Eugen Sandow 175
Adolph Nordquest 181
Joseph Vitole 187
Henry Steinborn 193
Bobby Pandour 213

INTRODUCTION

To the average young man there is no subject quite so fascinating as a discussion of physical strength. You can prove this to yourself any time you care to start a discussion among your friends. All you have to do is to remark that a certain acquaintance of yours is certainly the strongest fellow in town. Immediately all your friends will want to know just how strong he is, and each man present will insist that *he* knows a fellow who is "terribly strong." Claims and counter-claims will be made, and before you know it, the discussion will have taken a new turn, and those present will be talking about the great "Strong Men" of past and present time. You will be told of feats of strength performed by unknown men which would put Samson and Hercules in the class of the "also-rans," and you will hear of men so prodigiously developed that that giant, the late Louis Cyr, would have seemed small by comparison. Eventually and inevitably the talk will veer around to the question of "What makes a man strong?" and then you will hear some of the most fantastic beliefs and theories that the mind of man can conceive.

Among the uninformed, the general consensus of opinion is that either a "Strong Man" is "born strong" or else that he is in possession of some mysterious secret, or secrets, which account for his phenomenal strength.

How do I know all this? Well, because I have "listened in" on many such a confab. Why, once while on tour, I went to get shaved in the barber-shop of a small-

13

town hotel. The place being full I had to wait my turn. One of the other customers, while getting a hair-cut, was reading a copy of a well-known sporting paper and came across the picture of an amateur "Strong Man" lifting an apparently heavy weight. He showed the picture to his barber and soon all hands were engaged in the usual argument about strength and muscles. The names of great strength-athletes were mentioned, and, to my surprise I found that I had a champion. This lad said, "I tell you the strongest of the lot is that feller, Earle Liederman in New York." When pressed for his reasons he explained that he thought I had the "grandest arm" of them all.

Now, according to all the rules, that should have been the cue for me to step forward, roll up my sleeve so as to display the arm in question, and say, "Behold! I am he"— or something like that. Whereas what I actually did was to remain in the background and keep my mouth shut. For I know what these "Strong Man" fans are like. If I had butted into the conversation, they would have kept me there an hour answering their questions. There really is a tremendous curiosity about "Strong Men"—their lives, measurements, feats of strength, and particularly their methods of training.

A real "Strong Man" excites a great deal of interest and curiosity. When he is giving theatrical performances, there will always be a little crowd of young men who hang around the stage door and wait for him to come out, just so as to get a good look at him at close quarters.

(Just the way that these girl music-students do to the famous prima donnas.)

And if one chap picks up enough courage to accost the "Strong Man" and engage him in a few seconds' conversation, then that chap has something to brag about. In the future whenever the great athlete's name is mentioned, he will say, "Oh! I know *him*. Let's see! The last time I talked to him was when he was here at the————— Theater."

But, really, any great "Strong Man" will tell you that when on the road, he holds a continued reception. In the towns he visits local physical-culturists will ask for introductions to him, seek interviews with him, and beg for signed photographs. If an interview is granted, the visitor, after the usual expressions of regard and admiration, will say, *"Tell me, Mr. So-and-So, what did you do to get so strong?"*

Just as if the athlete, who has probably spent years in perfecting his body, could, in a few sentences, tell a beginner how to become equally strong and well-built!

But there it is. Notwithstanding the fact that the average young fellow, will in conversation, loudly proclaim his belief that all "Strong Men" are "born that way," and at the same time express the opinion that he— the speaker—could never become very strong, nevertheless, he has a secret conviction that if he only "knew the inside"—could find out the trade secrets—that he could be just as strong as the strongest of them all.

It would be impossible for me to tell you how many scores of thousands of health-seekers I have trained, but

I would be willing to bet that at least fifty thousand individuals have written me letters telling me to lay out their courses so as to make them as strong as possible. It is just as natural for a youth to wish to be powerfully developed and tremendously strong as it is for a girl to desire great beauty of face and form. But just the same it is impossible for me to describe the training of a "Strong Man" in one short letter, or in one brief interview, as it would be for a champion boxer to tell all the details of his art in a half hour's talk.

That was my main reason for writing this book. It gives me the opportunity to supplement the instructions I give in my courses. For when a man first starts his training, it is necessary to confine his work to definite exercises, which are designed to develop the individual muscles, to shape and strengthen the whole body, and to promote a feeling of health and well-being. The first few months of an exercise program are devoted to what you might call foundation work. Monotonous and tiresome (sometimes), but necessary if a structure of great strength is to be reared.

The acquisition of really great strength, that is to become as strong yourself as two or three ordinary men, is a problem which requires special training, patience and knowledge, particularly knowledge. Remember, the first thing asked of an expert is, "What shall I do to become strong?"

In another book of mine I gave a description of the various exercises used by "Strong Men" to develop their tremendous muscles. But every one who has given the matter any thought, realizes that there is more to strength-building than just exercise alone. If your body is to grow steadily—to develop from the undeveloped state of the average man, to the beautifully shaped and terrifically powerful physique of the real strength-athlete, you must learn to regulate your training so as to get that proper balance between exercise, recuperation (sleep) and nourishment which makes for the greatest possible progress.

I have associated so much with "Strong Men" that I have had every opportunity to observe and study both their physical characteristics and their training methods, Much of what I have learned is told in the pages of thi. book. At that, I feel that I have not told the half of its although if you will look at the chapter headings you will find that I have dealt with almost every factor relating to strength.

The fact of the matter is that these men most famous for their strength are not only immensely powerful, but are also what you might call "virtuosos" in the strength line. Most of them are experts (a) in the creation of muscle, (b) in the kind of training that at once creates and conserves energy, and (c) in the scientific application of power.

The amateur physical-culturist can, therefore, learn a great deal from the experience of the professional. I feel that I am qualified to speak with some authority on the methods of professionals because, in the first place, I was for several years before the public, doing a "strong-act" in vaudeville; in the second place because ever since my early manhood I have been intimately associated with many of the most famous "Strong Men" of modern times; and lastly, because I have been successful in the work of aiding thousands of men and boys to achieve the glory that goes with great physical strength.

It is quite natural that magazines devoted to physical training should be illustrated with pictures of finely developed men. But I can remember when, not so very many years ago, even the biggest magazines were lucky if in a single issue they could show pictures of even as many as half a dozen really well-built individuals. Nowadays the supply of such pictures is almost unlimited. Why, I myself issue periodically reports from my pupils, and each little folder shows the pictures of dozens of amateur pupils of mine; many of whom compare favorably in development and strength with the best professionals. In fact I have on hand enough unpublished pictures of fine physical specimens—contributed by my own pupils— to illustrate all the numbers of a magazine for years to come. Which, if it means anything, is some proof that I have had some success in handling strength cases, even if the bulk of my business is with individuals who are primarily health-seekers.

The seeker after great strength is necessarily in an advanced class. Usually he is a young fellow, who, having built up his body and increased his development rapidly through devotion to his daily exercise, comes to the point where he wishes to be able to exert the strength which is warranted by his big muscular body. He knows that his exercise has fully justified itself, because he feels better than ever before in his life. Besides that, his improved proportions have attracted a lot of attention and favorable comment. Especially, his muscles seem to excite curiosity; his friends remark on their size and shape; and usually wind up by expressing their belief that he must be very strong, and further asking him to display his strength. Quite naturally, the young athlete wishes to impress others by his strength as well as by his development. That is the stage which some of my ambitious pupils have reached when they write to me for further help and advice.

From their letters I can tell that what they expect is more and harder exercises. Whereas, what is really necessary is some tips on advanced methods of training. Such, for instance, as the necessity of building up great reserve energy through the avoidance of too much exercise. Or on the great importance of strengthening any weak links in the muscular chain. Or, perhaps, on the necessity of better (though not necessarily more) nourishment.

If, however, after diagnosing a pupil's needs, I were to sit down and write him a ten-page letter, dealing with any one of the three requirements above mentioned, he might be disappointed. For, instead of getting more exercises, he would be getting unexpected advice on just one phase of strength-creation. Because he would be getting only one angle he would be unable to see the whole picture— the subject in its entirety.

So, I decided to write a book in which I could present the whole subject; and give my pupils—and the public— a better understanding of the many details of muscular development, symmetry of body, quality of fibre, nerve force and athletic skill, which, when found or developed in one man, make him a physical super-man.

I have two great articles of belief, the first being that the average young man can become very much stronger than he has any idea of; and the second, that if an aspirant follows the advice given in the following pages he can attain great and permanent strength without any danger of overstrain, of staleness, or of loss of speed or energy.

I might even say that great strength is possible for *any* young fellow unless he happens to be helplessly crippled. Even those who are lacking in size, in vigor, or who suffer from minor diseases, can first overcome their weaknesses by the medium of corrective, developing and invigorating exercises; and then, after their bodies have become properly shaped and muscled, can acquire that great strength which is the crowning glory of true manhood. I have seen so many weaklings become "Strong Men" that I have become convinced that the capability for possessing great strength is within *all* of us. And that any man, however weak, can become *very* strong if he has the ambition, the persistence and the knowledge. While I cannot give you the first two, I feel that I can help out on the information.

I know "Strong Men" of almost every conceivable size and shape; from big-boned, massive giants, down to little "five-footers," who, though small-boned, are masses of muscle and energy. And, between those two extremes, men of all the intermediate stages of size, whose one common possession is that distinctive beauty of form and high degree of muscular development which marks the true "Strong Man."

So, in conclusion, if you are one of that ever-growing army of strength-enthusiasts, I can assure you that physical power *can* be yours; but that the road to strength is easier, and can be traveled quicker if you avoid the stumbling blocks, and keep out of the ruts. Here is hoping that some of the information given in this book will make the road smoother for you.

CHAPTER I

Inherited and Acquired Strength

Is there a secret of strength, and if so, what is it? That is what puzzles most seekers after athletic ability and physical perfection. So well-known a writer as Robert Edgren says that "Strength is where you find it," thus virtually claiming that great physical strength is "a gift" —pure and simple; and that either one has it—or one has to do without it.

The author of these chapters, being personally acquainted with hundreds of "Strong Men," and having been instrumental in helping thousands of men to attain great physical strength, believes that there is no such thing as "one great secret"; but a number of factors, or causes, which account for the surprising strength of some individuals; and that furthermore those factors are within the control of the individual, thus rendering it possible for any one who desires strength to obtain it.

The thoroughbred horse, an animal which is frequently cited as a sample of physical perfection, is not a product of nature, but of intelligent selection, breeding, and training. Man is responsible for the development of the thoroughbred animal, and it is a queer commentary on our ideals that the creating, or development, of thoroughbred animals—horses, cattle and dogs—is in some quarters regarded as more important than the developing of thoroughbred human beings.

A racing horse is bred and trained for speed; and by means of intelligent mating of parents, of feeding, of exercise and care there has been developed an animal superbly shapely with steel-spring muscles, and of certain marked characteristics. Literally characteristics—elements of character such as dauntless courage, stamina, and eagerness for work. By molding the body and physical attributes of the animal to the highest degree of perfection, the horse breeders and trainers have automatically produced mental or "character" attributes of the same high standard.

The horse has been simply clay in the hands of the potter, a docile instrument in the hands of the guiding force—man. Left to themselves horses would change, improve or develop very slowly. Horses have neither the intelligence nor initiative of mankind. It has taken probably twenty generations to produce the modern thoroughbred racer; but it is my opinion that, given equal care, all *men* could be molded to the thoroughbred type in two or three generations.

I will go even further than that. I believe that it is in the power of every man to make a marked improvement in his physical attributes, providing he will spend on himself but a fraction of the care that is spent in developing a high-grade animal.

There are unquestionably some men of gigantic strength who *inherit* their physical powers. The famous Canadian, Louis Cyr, stated that he got his strength and size from his mother, who was a woman of great size and most unusual power.

I know a physical director in New York City, a man of great all-round strength—but particularly famous for the strength of his hands and wrists—who tells me that his mother had the most powerful hands and wrists of any woman he had ever seen, and that she had more strength and vigor than most men.

Another clear case of inheritance. Apollon, the great Frenchman, who rivaled Cyr in strength, came of a family of circus-performers and "Strong Men," but he was vastly stronger than either of his parents or grandparents.

Out in Ohio there is a family named Nordquest, which numbers among its members some of the strongest men in modern history. The father is tall and well-made, but not markedly above the average in strength. The mother is small. Of the six sons, three of them, Arthur, Adolph and Joe are veritable Vikings in build, and marvels of muscular power. The other three sons are all naturally well-built and above the average in strength, but lack the prodigious power of the three more famous brothers. Arthur, Adolph and Joe are enthusiastic devotees of athletics and trained with the idea of becoming *supermen.* The other three have just the same inheritance, the same possibilities, and given the same training *might* quite possibly have become just as remarkable. All six had the possibilities; but the famous three voluntarily developed their possibilities; and their present power is unquestionably due to inheritance plus initiative—*the will to be strong.*

I could go on and tell you about dozens of other celebrities who frankly admit that their strength is inherited from one or both parents. I recall one present record-holding lifter who frankly says that while his own lifting power has been cultivated, that from his early boyhood he possessed great strength and that the male members of his family were always known as the strongest men in that particular part of Europe in which they lived. Consequently he was somewhat annoyed when one of our training concerns claimed that his strength was due to their system of exercises; although he admitted that he had cultivated and added to his inherited strength by following the same methods they advocated.

I know of an interesting case of another "muscle man" whose beautiful proportions and phenomenal strength are unquestionably due to his own efforts. His father and mother are far from being anything remarkable as physical specimens; and so far as his two brothers are concerned, one of them is short and stout, and the other short and thin. While the athlete himself is taller than the average, so strong that he created some amateur lifting records, and so beautifully shaped that he was in great demand as a sculptor's model; but then he was an "exercise devotee" and *worked* for his present physique, while his brothers were content to get along with such physique as they had inherited.

I am not attempting to minimize the value of a good inheritance. If your parents happen to be fine, straight, upstanding and vigorous physical specimens, and have passed on to you those desirable physical attributes, then you will find it just that much easier to develop a body that is the last word in physical perfection. But on the other hand you need not despair if it so happens that your parents are undersized or "just average." That makes it a little harder for you to become big and strong, but does not make it impossible. It will take you longer, that is all.

Everybody knows that certain families run true to a particular type. You may know a family of Joneses and whenever you speak of them you say, "All those Jones men are tall." In another family all the men may be stout, and in still other cases all the male members are very slender. In some powerful strains there are strongly marked characteristics which persist for generation after generation; as for example the Hapsburg lip, and the Bourbon nose.

There are people who are so impressed with the force of heredity that they can conceive of no other factor in the molding of the human body.

To them the Biblical query: "Can an Ethiopian

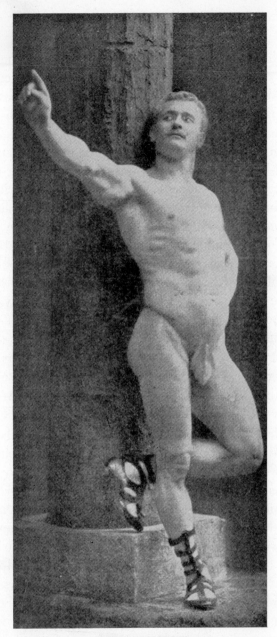

EUGEN SANDOW

The famous "column" pose that has been imitated
by numerous athletes but, as yet, has never been
duplicated. Sandow possessed a physique which
nobody could criticize but himself.

change his skin or a Leopard his spots?" is the final word. They overlook the fact there is a great difference between different Ethiopians and different Leopards. Of course, there are inherited characteristics which cannot be changed or altered in the individual. A blond Scandinavian cannot change himself into a brunet; nor can a round-headed man change himself into a long-headed man, for those are *race* characteristics. But when it comes to altering the form, or the appearance, or the strength of an *individual*, then use and environment are just as potent factors as heredity. Recently published statistics show that in Great Britain the average farm laborer is a couple of inches taller and nearly five pounds heavier than the average city mechanic; the superiority of the farm laborer being due to better food, more fresh air and more muscular work.

Charity-workers can furnish you with dozens of instances where puny, sickly, city children have made astonishing gains from even one month spent in the country, where they got plenty of food and outdoor play.

Hereditary physical characteristics persist only when generation after generation of the same family remain in the same environment and the same kind of employment. The sons of an undersized factory hand will grow big and strong if at an early age they are put at vigorous outdoor labor; and the sons of a husky farm-hand will remain weak and small if at an early age they are put to working twelve hours a day in a poorly ventilated mill or factory.

In his book "How to Get Strong," Wm. Blaikie unwittingly gave an illustration of such a case. He attempted to prove that many very famous men had been possessed of unusual physical strength. In some instances he made out a convincing case but in others failed to prove his point. As in his comment on Shakespeare, where he stated that Shakespeare had splendidly shaped legs; and all he had to go on was a *recent* statue of Shakespeare, where the sculptor had represented the poet as a man with a beautifully molded pair of lower limbs. All history proves that Shakespeare was a small and *slight* man.

Blaikie said, which is true, that Henry Ward Beecher was a man of imposing physique and great physical strength; and quoted Beecher himself to show that his size and strength were largely inherited. Mr. Beecher said that his father was so strong that he could lift a 400-pound barrel of cider a couple of feet from the ground; and that his grandfather could lift the same barrel to arms-length overhead and hold it there while drinking from the bunghole. Beecher came from New England farm folk, and if he had himself been a farmer instead of a preacher, the vigorous outdoor work might have made him as strong as his forbears. He inherited the vigor and the *possibilities* of strength, but not the gigantic strength itself. It is undeniable that we—all of us—inherit *some* possibility of strength. It would be easy to reverse the Beecher case. A small undersized city worker might move to the country and breed big upstanding children and these children in turn would produce a still better third generation, *if* they lived under ideal conditions as to food and outdoor exercise, or labor.

Those who claim that physical strength can only be inherited are being continually confronted with cases which disprove their theory. A young man will say "Oh yes! I am pretty strong. But you ought to see my father. He is nearly fifty and is twice as strong as I am." And if the father hears this he will chuckle, and say "Bill never had to do the hard work that I did."

On the other hand, I can introduce you to hundreds of young men who greatly exceed their fathers in size and strength. Largely because their fathers entered sedentary business pursuits at an early age, and were youths at a period when athletics were unpopular, and systematic exercise was regarded as a foolish waste of time.

Now, I myself am taller, bigger and *vastly* stronger than any of my male relatives on either side of the family. All of which I ascribe to my devotion to exercise and my love of the open air. When I work I work hard, and when I play I play hard. For weeks at a stretch I will spend twelve hours a day at my office, keeping myself in trim by eating sparingly, and allowing fifteen minutes daily to exercise.

The only reason I speak of myself is because I consider that I am a pretty good argument against the hereditary strength theory. I positively know that my present strength and development are due not to inherited advantages, but to my own efforts at self-improvement.

Such men as Henry Steinborn, Arthur Saxon, Cyr, Apollon and dozens of others undoubtedly inherited strength. Saxon said, "In boyhood I was always very much stronger than the average." Cyr at fifteen was stronger than two ordinary full-grown men.

On the contrary, Sandow has always claimed that he literally *made* himself strong and well-built. And other noted strength athletes make the same statement. Matysek, who is one of the best of American lifters, owes his superb figure and great strength to his consistent training. Thomas Inch, England's greatest strong man, is another who built himself up "from strength to strength." Starting to exercise when a boy, he developed himself into a beautifully shaped middle-weight Samson; and then *just to prove he could*, turned himself into a heavy-weight Hercules, by a few weeks of special training.

It must be admitted that if you are passionately interested in making yourself into a physical marvel, it is very discouraging to run up against these fellows who do inherit strength and who do not seem to have the least interest in cultivating that strength.

Old Colonel Higginson, in his time one of the most enthusiastic advocates of vigorous exercise, brought up this subject half a century ago—saying: "It is very discouraging when you have first learned to 'put up' a 50-pound bell, and after more training 'put up' 75 pounds, to see some big husky young fellow who never before touched a dumb-bell, step forward and 'put up' 100 pounds at his first attempt." It disheartens you, if after exercising and doing gymnastic work for a couple of years, and getting your biceps up to 14½ inches, you meet some splendidly built young fellow who carelessly displays a 16-inch arm, and when you ask how he got it, are told that "all his family have arms like that."

The son of a wealthy father, eventually inheriting the family wealth, rarely knows as much about the value of money, or how to make it, as did his father who earned it, or accumulated it. Similarly a man who inherits size and physical strength from his parents seldom realizes the value of his natural advantages, and almost never takes the trouble to improve or cultivate them. That explains why few celebrated "Strong Men" have sons who equal them in strength. Apollon was stronger than his father, but in most cases the opposite is the case. Athleta, the strongest woman in France, has three daughters doing "Strong Acts" on the vaudeville stage; but none of them are as strong as she is. I cannot recall the name of any "Strong Man" who has a son of equal strength.

Those who inherit strength seem disinclined to do that particular kind of hard work which alone produces enormous strength. Perhaps they find their strength sufficient, and never having been weak, have never experienced the craving for the fullness of physical power. Just as the son of a "captain of industry," who has never known what it is to need money, will not strive and scheme and work unendingly to amass a fortune the way his father did.

In the world of affairs, a certain respect is accorded to the "self-made man"; to the individual whose position is due entirely to his own energy, initiative, and ability. Such a man is master of his own fate. Why then should we not regard with equal respect the man, who, starting with a small and weak body, *builds himself up* until he is a model of manly strength and symmetry; whose shoulders are broad because he *made* them broad, whose back is powerful, strong because he made it so, and who has in general not merely grown stronger, but has literally *made himself* stronger. In some quarters there is a disposition to sneer at the "made" "Strong Man," and to glorify the man who inherited strength; whereas it seems to me that the credit should properly go to the man who achieves great strength through his own efforts.

Building muscle is not only my business but also my hobby. Years ago a chance meeting with a famous "Strong Man" planted in my breast the desire to be as strong as he was; and since that time I have missed no chance, spared no work to make myself stronger and better built. I am still improving, and at 37 years of age am considerably stronger, and have far more "pep" and energy than I had when I was thirty. What I accomplished through toil and pains, *you* can do with less trouble and less effort. It took me years to find out just what was

GEORGE HACKENSCHMIDT

The famous wrestler who created records in lifting. His 52-inch chest, 22-inch neck and 19-inch biceps are seen to advantage in the above pose.

the best combination of exercise, and rest and food, for producing big results; but having acquired that knowledge I am ready to pass it on to you in the pages of my various books, and through the medium of my courses of instruction.

There are certain races or nations which seem to abound in strong men. One authority claims that the French-Canadians produce more giants of strength than any other race. Others claim that the Finns are physically the strongest nation.

The Balkan nations produce scores of natural "Strong Men," and for that matter so do the Turks, and the "Tartars" of Western Asia; the latter being known to neighboring tribes, by a word which means "The Strong Men." It should be noted that all of the foregoing inhabit countries in which most of the work is still done by man-power; where machinery is scarce, and few work indoors; where men have to use their muscles of necessity. And there is the whole secret of strength. *Use* your muscles and they will grow continually stronger. A man who allows his body machinery to rust through lack of use, has no more chance of realizing his full strength than a tree has to grow if it is planted in a place which gets no sunlight.

But if work, muscular exertion, were the only requisite for producing strength then every day-laborer should be a Hercules; which, of course, is far from being the case. There are three principal reasons why the average workman is not very strong. The *first* being that he has *too* much work, being forced to continue after he is tired, with the consequence that he destroys tissue faster than he can rebuild it. *Second*—That only few employments require the use of all the muscles, and all-round development is the prime requisite of great bodily strength.

Third—It is but rarely that work or labor requires the extreme contractions and the vigorous effort which produce muscles of great size and high quality. A teamster, or truckman, who spends ten minutes in lifting, hauling and pushing into place immensely heavy bales and boxes, and then has an hour of comparative rest while he drives these boxes to their destination, will become very much stronger than the workman who handles comparatively light packages for hours without rest.

If strength, shapeliness and health could be obtained only by taking a job as a laborer, then very few would be willing to sacrifice their financial welfare for the sake of health and strength. Happily, it has been proved, that a short period of daily exercise, *of the right sort*, will give a man greater strength, a better shape and better health than he could possibly get by labor. In any well-thought-out exercise program, care is taken to provide developing and conditioning work for every part of the body; whereas in labor the work is apt to be done by comparatively few muscles. Also in an exercise program it is possible to include exercises which enlarge the lungs, which strengthen the heart, and which invigorate the digestive organs. Best of all, an exercise program provides against over-exertion, and helps one to build up a store of reserve energy—all of which subjects are dealt with in the following chapters.

There are so very few men who are *extremely* strong that it sort of knocks out the theory that great strength is an inherited attribute. There are *big* men by the thousands, *heavy* men by the tens of thousands, but really *strong* men are rare. Possibly not one man in a thousand is so strong as to be in a class *far* above the average; and great, or unusual strength is a possession that it is impossible to conceal. For people worship strength in a man even more than they admire beauty in a woman. You, who are reading these words, probably are acquainted with at least one hundred men and boys whom you meet in a business or social way. If you are inclined to athletics, or devoted to some outdoor sport, it is possible that you know a hundred *athletes;* men who are physically better than the average. And yet how many out of that hundred are distinguished for their strength? Probably not more than one or two. A big university may have five or six thousand students, including scores of oarsmen, football players and track athletes; and yet not more than five or six of these young men are strong enough to make really good records in such strength stunts as "putting the shot" and "throwing the hammer." If a youth while in college displays enormous strength, his feats and power will become a college tradition, and his name will be mentioned with awe; and it is but seldom that investigation develops that such an athlete is the son of a very strong father. If such were the rule, it would mean that strength was a monopoly of a very few individuals, and that a strong man who had inherited a fixed amount of strength from his father would in his turn pass on exactly that amount of strength to his sons. Fortunately for most of us, nature does not work in that way. What then would be the use of any one trying to improve himself in any way? These believers in the hereditary theory overlook the great constructive forces of environment, ambition, and initiative. *Your* father and grandfather may have been small and weak men; but that is no more reason for *you* to remain small and weak, than for you to remain poor because they happened to lack money. In the cultivation of the body there is no truer principle than "Nature helps him who helps himself."

I got so interested in this subject of heredity that I put the question to all the "Strong Men" whom I happen to know personally; and out of several dozen only a few of them could truthfully say that either, or both, of their parents had been very strong. Just as you could do, I can cite families where every law of heredity seems to be defied; where one daughter will be beautiful and another extremely homely; where two brothers are puny and two others are big and brawny; where all the children are taller than either parent; or where they are shorter. I know one case where the father is five feet eight inches tall and the mother only five feet two and they have a son who stands six feet four in his stocking feet. And I know a Herculean man—a former oarsman and football player—whose cross in life is that his full-grown son is one of these round-shouldered, flat-chested lounge-lizards.

Like everyone else I believe in the value of a good physical inheritance, but just the same I can find no conclusive evidence that physical strength is purely an inherited trait. Once I thought I had tracked down a case of inherited strength, but investigation found that I was mistaken.

At that time I lived in a residential district and near me was quite a large church. I soon noticed the particular deference paid to the pastor of that church by the boys and young men of the neighborhood. If a crowd was hanging around a corner and this minister approached, the word would be passed around "Here he comes"; and every boy would brace himself up, step forward and try to catch the minister's eye. And if the minister, as he usually did, would give a friendly nod and greeting, they would be visibly proud at being remembered and would watch him until he was out of sight. Having seen this happen several times with different groups of young fellows, I got curious and asked one crowd whether they all belonged to that man's church. "No! none of them did." "Why, then," I asked, "did they make such a fuss over him? Was he a celebrated preacher or what?" Immediately I was overwhelmed with information. According to these youths the preacher was certainly the strongest man in the whole city. One of them had seen him break a three-inch stick of wood as though it were a walking stick; another had seen him carry a huge section of a steam-heater, and so on. He had a gymnasium in his parish house and once in a while he would join the boys and entertain them by joining in a "tug of war," and at one end of the rope would pull around a dozen youths at the other end.

This preacher (I cannot even remember his name or what denomination he belonged to) was a man of middle size, not over five feet eight inches in height and weighing probably 180 pounds. His shoulders were not very broad but were exceedingly thick; his chest was deep from front to back and his back was wide and even the clerical cut of his clothes could not conceal the fact that he had a tremendously powerful pair of legs. Here, I thought, is a man who *must* have inherited his strength, for certainly there is nothing in a preacher's way of living to make a man as strong as that. So I asked for an interview and frankly explained my interest and curiosity.

He said "Yes, I suppose I am very strong, and sometimes I wish I wasn't, because it is not quite seemly for a minister of the gospel to be respected more for his muscles than for his preaching. But then, it gives me quite a lot of influence with the boys, and that is a good thing. Was my father strong? Oh no, not particularly so. He was a poor country doctor and I had to work my own

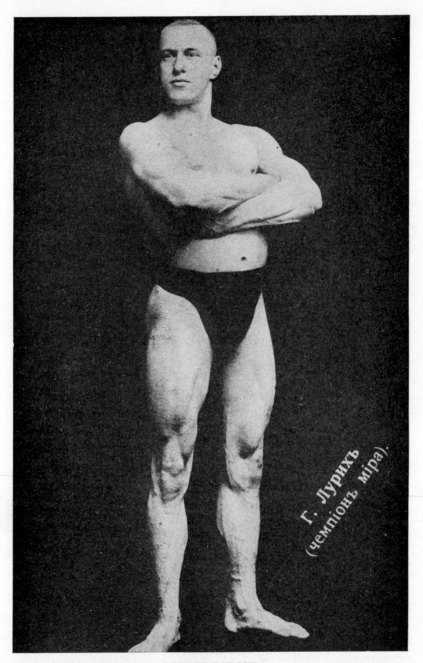

Г. Лурихъ
(чемпіонъ міра).

GEORGE LURICH

The famous wrestler and lifter. Besides possessing enormous strength he was exceptionally quick of movement, thereby proving that strong men are not necessarily slow of action.

way through divinity school. I supported myself and paid my college bills by working in a lumber yard. I made an arrangement so that I would be paid by piece-work. I worked hard and would earn as much in two or three hours as the ordinary workman could make in a day. The harder I worked the stronger I got, and after a while I got so that I could carry and stack pieces of lumber that two ordinary men could not even lift. Look at my hands, they will tell you the story." And sure enough his hands were those of a man who had done hard work. Big and broad, and thick fingered; and I could believe him when he said he could crack black walnuts with his fingers and thumbs. And there the conversation ended because the man was obviously embarrassed at having to talk about his body. It was just one more case where strength was due to a man's own efforts and will power; and another proof of how vigorous work *in regulated quantities* produces a vigorous body. I dare say the man was a fine preacher and a good man and all that; but what made him such an influence among the youth of the district was his fearsome physical power. It would have been just the same if he had happened to be a lawyer or a store-keeper or a policeman.

The reason why people thus admire a "Strong Man" is that such strength is so very uncommon. Out of a thousand women, a couple of hundred will be noticeably good-looking and half a dozen will be real beauties, but not *one* man in a thousand has the tremendous strength that sets him apart, and above, his fellow men.

There were a lot of judges in Israel but the only one the average person can name was Samson; and while most people know that he killed a thousand men in one combat and pulled down a temple, few can tell you one thing he did in his professional capacity as a judge.

Chapter II

Power and Strength
(*Influence of size and weight*)

You are walking along the street with a friend, you meet some big husky of the Jim Jeffries type and your friend exclaims admiringly, "My, what a powerfully built chap!"

Now you can just picture the kind of man that is "powerfully built." Usually he is about six feet tall, broad-shouldered, big-chested, wide-hipped, with sturdy legs and thick arms. He looks as though he could *do* a lot; which is why you call him powerful. Power involves action, movement.

Power can be derived from momentum. A stream of water coming through a two-inch pipe through a drop of 200 feet will develop more power than a much thicker stream falling only a few feet. Momentum is weight multiplied by speed. Therefore a big man who can move quickly can ordinarily exert more power than a small man moving at equal speed; that is, if each of the two is fairly strong and well-knit.

Size alone does not make a man powerful; he must have strength along with his bulk. A fat man might be 5 feet 10 inches tall and weigh 275 pounds, and yet not be powerful at all. Most of his weight would be made up of soft flesh, which has not the driving power of well-conditioned muscle; and which further interferes with his freedom of movement, and makes any speed impossible. Most "fat men" are far from being powerfully built, although their very weight enables them to exert *some* power in certain limited ways.

41

To illustrate—Some years ago one of the most popular characters at a certain seaside resort was a real "fat man." He was nearly six feet tall and weighed over 400 pounds in his bathing-suit. In fact he was so stout that he could get in and out of a taxicab door only by having two friends push and pull him. He was a great mixer, and not in the least sensitive about his abnormal size. He would join the boys on the beach and pass the medicine ball and play catch. You know the way they work it. Half a dozen fellows will get in one group and as many more in a group fifty yards away. They throw a tennis ball from crowd to crowd, and whoever is nearest catches the ball and returns it. Sometimes several fellows rush to the spot where the ball is about to land; shouldering one another out of the way— so as to have the fun of making the catch and return throw. Well—whenever this big fat chap wanted to make the catch he was allowed to do so. If any foolhardy fellow reached the spot at the same instant he would simply cannon off that mountain of a man like a billiard ball from a cushion. But that was where the fat man's power ended. He could not throw the ball back again. Nor could he in any other way exert a fraction of the strength which we would naturally expect from a man of his size. He could not lift a heavy weight from the ground nor carry anything heavy. Neither could he hit a hard blow. A really muscular man weighing 400 pounds would be inconceivably powerful; and as we all know, even a *fairly* muscular man weighing 250 pounds can be very powerful. This applies especially in personal combat; in man-to-man stunts where one man's weight and strength is opposed to another's. It is hard to appraise the strength of the contestants in most combats because skill has been developed to such a point that it is a tremendous factor.

An expert wrestler, even though he be a middleweight, can make a monkey out of a greenhorn of twice his own weight. But let us suppose that there are two wrestlers equally skilful, one weighing 225 pounds and the other 150 pounds. Undoubtedly the extra power of the bigger man would make him the winner—because during the match he would be handling a man only two-thirds of his own weight—while the smaller man would have the extra exertion of trying to heave around a man who out-weighed him by fifty per cent. That is, the big man's work would be easy and the small man's very hard. The outsider is apt to forget the question of comparative weights, but the professional knows that weight counts—which is why a 135-pound boxer draws the line at meeting a good 140-pounder.

Nobody is foolish enough to expect a light-weight boxer to defeat a good heavy-weight—because they know that a good fighter has to have the knack of getting all his weight behind a blow. If Dempsey and Leonard were fighting and both landed on the other at exactly the same instant—then Dempsey with his weight would have all the advantage.

To apply power the athlete must have speed, skill, balance, weight and strength. A football line-coach will spend hours in teaching a candidate just how to manage his body and control his weight so that he is able to out-charge an opponent. Just as no fat man is really powerful, so no *awkward* man can display much power, simply because he cannot control his body and limbs so as to get the maximum work out of them.

From the foregoing it would sound as though no small or medium-sized man, no matter how strong, would have any chance in a test of strength and power against even a fairly good big man. Happily such is not the case, be-

cause there are men of medium size who have such terrific strength and energy that they are able to put as
much power into a movement as are even the best of the
big ones. This applies especially in tests where the body
is at rest, or when it moves slowly.

I saw an exemplification of this one afternoon when a
lot of very famous wrestlers, lifters, and heavyweight
athletes were indulging in an impromptu contest at
"wrist-wrestling." In this stunt the competitors sit on
either side of a table facing each other, place their right
elbows on the table-top, grasp each other's right hand,
and then each man tries to force his opponent's arm down
until the back of former's hand rests on the table. Since
the competitors are forced to sit bolt upright, with their
left forearms resting in front of them on the table, it is
impossible to use the weight of the body as a factor, and
so the whole thing is a test of pure strength in the wrist
and arm.

Among the crowd were athletes of all sizes up to a
couple of gigantic 250-pound wrestlers. But the man
who won was a little chap who stood only 5 feet 4 inches
and weighed only 145 pounds. He was what you might
call a "pocket-Hercules"; and although he was so short,
his chest was nearly as big and his arms as powerfully
muscled as those of the largest men present. He was
particularly strong in his arm flexors—the muscles which
bend the arm at the elbow—and which bend the palm of
the hand towards the forearm—and so naturally he was
good at stunts such as "chinning the bar" and "curling"
heavy weights. So it was not surprising that he should be
good at "wrist wrestling"—and he was *too* good for the
rest of them. Not even the biggest and heaviest man
there could push his hand even a trifle backwards, while
he could put their arms down as fast as they came.

EDWARD ASTON

The famous British middle-weight lifter, who bent-pressed over 300 pounds, one
hand overhead. Another example of what secrets of strength can be stored up in
one human dynamo.

One would think that a powerful man would of necessity be very strong, but such is not always the case. In most of the big universities the physical departments hold periodic "strength tests" where each student is required to exert his full strength in pulling, pushing or lifting against the resistance of various machines, which resist the athlete's efforts and register the force of his muscles. The chap who makes the highest total on the machines is known as the "strongest man in college." It sometimes happens that the winner is some giant football player, but in such instances it usually happens that he is known as the "strong man" of the squad. But just as often the winner is some middle-sized student who has never won a name in athletics; but by devotion to gymnastic and developing exercises, has acquired a set of muscles that enable him to exert enormous strength.

So far as I know the strength record for all the colleges is in the possession of "Mike" Dorizas, of the University of Pennsylvania. Dorizas was a football player, a weight-thrower and intercollegiate champion wrestler; but his greatest claim to athletic fame is his reputation as a "strong man." Although no bigger or heavier than many other football players, Dorizas was admittedly twice as strong physically as most football men. He was not only powerful but tremendously strong—two things which seemed to be identical, but are not always so.

Undoubtedly the possession of immense muscular strength adds to the power of a big man; while in a small or medium sized man it compensates for lack of bulk and height.

The colored fighter, Joe Wolcott, weighed but 145 pounds, but was enormously strong and such a terrific hitter that he was known as the "Giant Killer"; and very few of the best of the big men would consent to fight him.

There have been others like him. A century ago in England there was a 140-pound pugilist who was supposed to be able to hit as hard as any man of his time. His supporters admitted that he was too light to be successful against the heavy-weights, but offered to back him against any man in the world, if both fighters were strapped straddled on a bench, facing each other. In that position the bodily weight was nullified, and the only thing that counted was sheer strength and hitting power.

I contend that a short man of moderate weight can exert enormous power, providing he is terribly strong, extra well-knit and has great speed and energy. I believe it is true that an experienced foreman will pick out big fellows for heavy labor; on the general principle that a large man can shift and lift more weight, and stick at it longer than a small man can. But I have seen men of moderate size who could stick on the job for hours at a time and do as much work as any man. When I hear stories of this, or that, man doing a huge day's work, I always think of a friend of mine who is a star in that respect. As a boy and young man he was intensely interested in gymnastics and feats of strength. He was one of those who cared more about what he was able to do than about his measurements and appearance. He trained on the gymnastic apparatus, used weights, and wrestled; but always picked out the kind of exercise that made him *use* his strength and his power. When in training he never weighed more than 140 pounds, but was so strong that he could lift and carry more than any one else of his size, and as much as the really big men could manage. He became particularly adept at applying his strength, and made quite a study of the most advantageous positions which would enable him to apply his power with the greatest force and the least expenditure of effort. After a time he married and retired from active athletics, but never lost his interest. At present he is about forty, has several children and runs a large trucking business. He employs a number of very husky drivers, but whenever there is a job which scares the others he steps in and does it himself. He undertook a contract for unloading and hauling four freight-car-loads of chemicals in iron drums —each drum weighing between five and six hundred pounds. He took one truck himself and put two of his biggest men on each of two other trucks, and actually he loaded, delivered and unloaded two car-loads of drums *single-handed*, sooner than the other two crews each did a car-load. In other words he did more work then the other four men. When asked to explain, he said that his years of exercise had so strengthened and hardened his muscles, and taught him so much about applying the weight of his body that with him it was simply a question of endurance; that he could keep on for hours doing things that an ordinary workman could do only a few times.

In other words, that while the average husky would have to cry for a rest after five minutes of hustling 500-pound bales or cases, this man could keep it up indefinitely; all the while working without much apparent exertion and no visible fatigue.

Power, therefore, is not the exclusive prerogative of big men. No man proved that more conclusively than the veteran athlete, John Y. Smith of Boston. Smith was a man who never weighed more than 168 pounds, yet he could do anything in the line of strength and power which could be accomplished by the natural giants. Although a dumb-bell-lifter by preference, he was one of those men who could lift or carry *anything*. It is told that once he passed some porters who were loading a truck with 200-pound bags of cement. Smith being in a jovial mood, stopped, and joked the men about the fuss they made over handling "little bags like those." Whereupon the men grew indignant and informed him that "it takes a man to handle these *heavy* bags," and invited him to take off his coat and see for himself whether it was as easy as he thought. Without taking off his coat, Smith seized one of the bags, swung it to his shoulder, and then slowly pushed it to arm's-length over his head. Having thus surprised the others, he proceeded to amaze them by taking the bags, two at a time, one in each hand, and *throwing* them into the truck.

One of his most noteworthy feats was to walk for 200 yards, while carrying in each hand a dumb-bell weighing over 200 pounds. Almost any husky workman or football player could walk that distance carrying 400 pounds on his back and shoulders; but to walk with that weight dangling from the ends of the arms is several times as hard as carrying the same weight on the back.

There is nothing that fascinates me so much as studying "Strong Men" and trying to figure out where all their physical force comes from. That is why this question of strength and power interests me. It would hurt me to have to admit that only big men can be "powerful" because that would seem to put a premium on mere size and bulk. Yet it has to be admitted that there are strength sports in which bulk is a distinct advantage. For instance, if I were the coach of a football team, and I knew that a rival team had a 220-pound guard who was plowing through all opposition, I would be tempted to put my biggest and heaviest man opposite him, instead of taking a chance with a light man, no matter how skilful. And yet there have been cases where light men have successfully held the line against big men. If I were coaching a track team or needed a hammer-thrower I would be apt to hunt around for some big, broad-shouldered, long-armed, thick-legged fellows, and train them; instead of wasting my time trying to make hammer-throwers out of lightweights, or even middle-weights.

Perhaps there is no sport which so well illustrates this mysterious difference between strength and power as does the throwing of weights. It seems that while it takes strength to lift or carry weights, it takes power to throw them. And that power is, or seems to be, dependent on the respective weight of the man and the object he throws. A good strong middleweight can make quite a success of "shot putting," because the weight, or shot, is "pushed" away from the body at the final moment, the body and arm traveling in the line of the "put," with the consequence that there is no bodily exertion necessary to counter-balance the moving weight. There have been men weighing in the neighborhood of 160 to 165 pounds who have put the 16-pound shot, 46 and even 48 feet. Nevertheless the only men who have put the shot out around 50 feet are the actual physical giants. In throwing the hammer, the weight which is at the end of a four-foot wire handle is first whirled around the head to get up impetus, and then the athlete allows his body to pivot with the whirling weight, making two, three, or four complete turns as he crosses the seven-foot circle; and finally discharges the weight on its journey with one final heave into which he puts all his weight and power. Naturally it is easier for a big and heavy man to keep his poise when whirling a hammer than it would be for a small and light man. The more rapidly you swing the weight the more momentum it attains, and the more it tends to pull you off your balance. The lighter you are

JOSEPH NORDQUEST

A striking pose of this remarkable strong man. His arms appear short owing to their enormous size, 18 inches, while in reality his reach is the same as his height, 68 inches.

the harder it is to resist the pull of the weight. I can conceive of a small man, weighing, say 125 pounds, who
could be strong enough to *stand still* and "keep his feet,"
while swinging the weight rapidly; but as soon as he
would revolve his body with the weight, he would be
pulled along with it, and would be dragged out of the
circle by the flying hammer. If he kept in the circle he
would get but little distance to his throw. So far as I
know, all the record-breaking hammer-throwers are big
men. I doubt if any man weighing less than 165 pounds
could become a star in that event. For a while the cham-
pionship was held by a succession of Irishmen, not one of
whom weighed less than 225 pounds, but in late years
our colleges have produced a number of young Ameri-
cans, who are equaling the records of the foreign stars;
and these young chaps are not so terribly big. Some of
them are six-footers, and others are only of middle
height. They weigh from 175 to 210 pounds, and what
they lack in bulk and sheer brawn, they make up for in
skill and energy.

The fact that weight is needed to *throw* weight is so
well recognized that in our schools the boys are made to
use 12-pound, and even 8-pound hammers; the heavy 16-
pounder being too apt to strain them.

Throwing the 56-pound weight is even more strenuous
than throwing the 16-pound hammer. The method of
throwing is somewhat the same, except that of course the
weight is not whirled around the head. But in order to
get momentum, the athlete has to hold the weight away
from his body and revolve the body itself, making two or
three complete turns as it crosses the circle.

To throw 56 pounds even a few feet away from you
requires both strength and practice, and is far easier for
a big man than for a small one. If the athlete weighs 224

pounds himself, then the weight is only one-quarter of his own; whereas if the athlete weighs 168 pounds it means that the weight is a third of his own; and you can realize how much easier it is to throw one-quarter of your weight than one-third of it. I doubt whether even the possession of great muscular strength would enable a middle-sized man to throw a 56-pound weight as far as could a bigger, but less strong, man.

Of course, some of these weight throwers *are* immensely strong as well as extremely big. It is told that a generation ago a visiting Irish athlete, who weighed over 250 pounds, on one occasion took a 56-pound weight in his right hand, whirled it around his head and, without moving his feet, tossed the weight 29 feet. It is hard for the average man to realize the amount of strength necessary to do a stunt like that one, because the average man cannot lift 56 pounds to the level of the crown of his head, much less swing it around as though it were an empty basket.

A similar feat is told of a man named Condon (or Coudon), who was one of the greatest hammer-throwers of the last generation. In his time they used the old-fashioned hammer, the one with a three-foot *wooden* handle. He could take such a hammer in one hand, whirl it a couple of times, and throw it a hundred feet with a single arm-motion. A friend of mine who knew him tells me that Condon's upper arm was as big as an ordinary man's thigh, and that besides being big he was prodigiously strong.

I admire strength and I get a real thrill out of seeing some man perform a feat that requires terrific strength, and I don't care whether it is lifting a huge bar-bell the way some of these stage performers do, or whether it is supporting on the shoulders a ton of live weight, as is done by the Arab tumblers. Recently I heard of a comparatively small man carrying single-handed a 1500-pound bathtub up a flight of stairs. This sounds incredible to me, but if I had seen it done, it certainly would have been something to remember and talk about.

I know that many of you who read this book have puzzled your brains trying to reconcile different kinds of feats of strength, and trying to decide where one kind of stunt requires more strength than another. One of my pupils recently said to me, "Mr. Liederman, I wish you would explain something to me. I have been reading your book about 'Strong Men,' and I realize that these 'Strong Men' are several times as powerful as the average athlete. The measure of their strength seems to be how much they can lift in one way or another. But why is it that these men do not take up weight-throwing and break all the records? You told us of several men who could 'put up' a 300-pound weight with the right arm. The arm muscles used in putting up a weight are the same ones that are used in putting the shot. A fellow that can 'put up' 300 pounds ought to be a wonder at shot-putting. Why I know some fellows who can put the shot over 40 feet and none of them can possibly 'put up' 125 pounds, let alone 300—it seems queer to me. Did you ever see any of these 'Strong Men' try shot-putting —and if so did they do anything wonderful?"

Now that is a fair question, and one that should be answered—but all I could tell my friend was that I had rarely seen a weight-lifter attempt to throw weights, nor a weight-thrower attempt to lift weights. I do remember one youth who was quite good as a lifter and who tried shot-putting. As I recall him he weighed 140 pounds and he could "put up" 210 pounds by what lifters call the one-arm bent press. That is a feat which requires great skill and balance as well as pushing power, and is not really a test of arm strength. This same youth, when he stood upright, could not push 100 pounds slowly aloft. I think 90 pounds was about his limit. Although he practiced several weeks he did not put the shot any further than 39 feet, and realizing that that was not good enough, he gave up the game, disgustedly remarking that he was neither tall enough or heavy enough to make a good shot-putter. Yet he was remarkably strong, not only in the arms but in the back and legs. Once I saw him load on the tail-board of a wagon a 600-pound casting which two other men had failed to put in position. On the other side I have often wondered how some of these big weight-throwers would show up in a test at bar-bell and dumb-bell lifting. It seems to me that a really husky 200-pound man should not have much trouble in "putting up" a 100-pound dumb-bell—that is, in the military position, with body erect and all the pushing, or lifting, done by arm strength. And the same thing should be true of the big weight-throwers. I understand that Cameron, the big Scotch hammer-thrower, once visited a weight-lifting club in London. He watched the members heaving around bar-bells, and when asked his opinion, grunted, and said that anyone could lift those bells. This nettled the lifters and they challenged him to have a try. After a heated argument he walked over, picked up the biggest bar-bell in the place (one that only a few members could lift overhead even when using both arms), grasped it in his two hands, pulled it to his chest, pushed it aloft and then taking a step forward, threw it over the top of a nearby partition. It must be remembered that Cameron was a giant of a man—celebrated as a wrestler and hammer-thrower, weighing at least 240 pounds and boasting a 48-inch chest and 18-inch biceps. That is one of the few cases I have heard of where a star at one game proved equally supreme in the other variety.

I have my own ideas about the source of strength and the creation of power—and I intend to elaborate those ideas in the following chapters.

But before I leave this subject I wish to say that I am in favor of the kind of strength that enables its possessor to use it in *any* kind of muscular work, be it sport or actual labor. In other words I believe that a man who is really strong should be able by virtue of his strength, to lift weights or carry them; to pull a strong oar in a crew; to plunge through the resistance offered by two or three opposing football players—to throw weights, to do difficult gymnastic stunts such as climbing the bar with one hand, or vaulting a seven-foot fence—to swing a heavy hammer all day without tiring—to carry huge trunks or bales, and to do *all* these things without special preparation or training, simply *because of the strength and energy that is in him*. At least, that is the kind of strength I try to give to those whom I train.

Chapter III

Strength through Muscular Development

Football used to be considered as a game only for huskies—but nowadays the coaches say that there is a place on the team for any man, no matter how small he is, providing he has the grit and the endurance, the speed and the energy.

So I say that a man can become strong no matter how much nature has handicapped him by giving him a lack of inches, or a small frame. Even those in ill-health can be made strong, because exercise promotes health. In turn muscle can be made to grow on the healthy body, and with muscle will come strength.

Some of the strongest men I know are little fellows; that is, little so far as height goes, for in every other way they are miniature giants. And most of them are strong today because they got tired of being snubbed and imposed on for their lack of inches and their dearth of strength.

Almost anyone who earnestly desires to, can make himself strong; not just ordinarily strong, but very much stronger than the average man, little or big. And to become strong—to add size and strength to your body, or in other words to develop it—takes much less time than to cultivate the mind.

A boy who enters school at eight years and graduates at eighteen, has during that ten years given up at least six hours a day to exercising and cultivating his mind. There was a time when those who run the schools gave no thought whatever to the cultivation of the body, but during the last generation the necessity of physical exercise has been recognized, and today the heads of schools see

to it that their pupils are compelled to take part in
sports, games and exercises which make for bodily betterment.

Undeniably, the brain can stand more work than the
body can. A student can spend four hours in the class
room and four more in concentrated study, without becoming brain-tired; in fact, his mental powers are *developed* by such application. The same student could not
spend eight hours per day at equally hard physical work
without becoming exhausted. Two hours of vigorous
play every day is sufficient to promote healthy bodily
growth in a schoolboy, while half of that is plenty enough
to keep a college student in condition.

But play—athletic sports and games—admirable as
they are, are neither the only nor the best means of physical education. Especially is this true at institutions where
sport is systematized, and the big teams get most of the
attention. For there the weak boy or youth, the one who
most needs the exercise and the physical training, has
to step aside and make room for the other boy who is
already so good that his presence on the playing field is
an asset to the institution.

At many colleges and schools, physical drill is required; but the very fact that it is compulsory robs it of
much of the value. "Setting up" exercises are better
than nothing, but when performed under compulsion
and in a haphazard way by a large group they tend to
become a monotonous hardship instead of an invigorating pastime.

Little or no effort is made to explain to the individual
student his own capacities for bodily improvement, nor
to awaken in him the desire for physical perfection.

For those who are interested in some particular sport,
every facility is provided. High-salaried coaches will

ARTHUR SAXON
A remarkable photograph of the late strong man, performing his official
world's record lift of 448 pounds in the two hand anyhow.

teach him all they know about how to play some game, and his hours for study will be arranged so as not to interfere with his hours for game practice. Members of teams are given special privileges. Under this system all that is required of the *non*-athletic student is that he shall appear regularly in the cheering section.

Anyone interested in the physical betterment of the rising generation cannot help being struck with the popularity of the playground as compared with the unpopularity of the gymnasium. The only time most students voluntarily go to the gym is when there is a chance to see a basketball game, or a boxing or wrestling tournament.

A student cannot graduate from school or college without passing specified tests, and to pass those tests proves that he has more knowledge and brain-power than at the beginning of his school work. I believe that it is possible to devise a system of physical education that will be just as successful in developing the physique of the pupil as the present system improves his mind.

But at present the weak and undeveloped man who wishes to become strong and healthy has to have recourse to the services of private teachers who will give him the kind of individual training his case demands. And such people are legion. Why, I myself in the course of a little over one year, heard from nearly half a million men and boys whose letters proved that they were interested in getting bigger, better and healthier bodies.

I mention that not as an instance of my own popularity, but as evidence of the tremendous and widespread interest in the cultivation of the body. Those letters came from all kinds and classes of citizens, all the way from the middle-aged business men who wished to regain their youthful figures and energy, down to college students and schoolboys who were after results which they could not obtain through the facilities afforded by the physical departments of their own institutions.

It has come to be recognized that systematic physical training will do as much for the body as systematic study will do for the mind. More and more people are becoming interested in acquiring for themselves beautiful, shapely, strong and healthy bodies.

And interest is the secret of development. Any teacher will tell you that a boy will learn vastly more about a subject in which he is interested, than in a subject which bores him. As a teacher of physical culture I can assure you that a man or boy who is *interested* in seeing how much strength and muscular development he can obtain, will improve in both respects ten times as rapidly as the other individual who looks upon exercise as a necessary nuisance, which must be done for health's sake.

There are many who are what you might call fatalists about their own bodies. They think that development "just happens," that either you have strength, or you haven't and that it is flying in the face of nature to try and increase your own physical assets.

I have in mind two brothers of exactly opposite types, both physically and mentally. The younger of the two, a tall, rangy youth of twenty-one, became dissatisfied with what he called his "scrawniness" and embarked on a system of home training that called for a half-hour's daily exercise of a rather rigorous character. The older brother, who was also tall but much broader-shouldered and heavier all-round, was inclined to sneer and jibe. He said to me, "I don't care what you say—strength doesn't come that way! Why look at me—when I was a kid I worked every summer on a farm. I would start in at six o'clock in the morning and work until supper time. Nearly twelve hours every day at plowing, reaping, spading, hoeing and all kinds of hard work. No wonder I have big shoulders and a strong back. My arms and legs are not very big, but then I have small bones. I feel that I have as much muscle and strength as nature intends me to have, and I think that Ed is a fool to think he can get even as big as I am by monkeying a little while every day with those 'exercisers.' Why, he never did any hard work in all his life. Let him do what I did and he can get strength if he wants it so badly."

Now, happily that younger brother was one of the kind that is not easily discouraged. He just went on quietly at his exercise, studying his weak points, and learning how to build them up. Also he had very definite ideas of just what he wanted to accomplish. For instance, he knew that in order to be well-proportioned he should have a 43-inch chest, and although his chest measured only 36 inches when he started, he knew that it was possible to get a chest as big as he wanted, because he knew of other men who had made that much improvement. To make a long story short, the younger man *did* get just the development he wanted (and the strength also) and now instead of being known as "the skinny boy" he is known as "that big, finely built boy." In fact, he now exceeds his older brother in development and strength just as much as he was inferior to him a year ago. But then he felt in his heart and soul *that it was possible* for him to improve. He refused to admit that while other men could build up, he could not. While the older brother who declined to make the effort necessary for improvement, now contents himself by insisting that there was "something unnatural" about Ed's growing so much huskier after he was twenty-one.

While I am on the subject, I can not help saying that

I am continually puzzled by the attitude some people have towards strength and development.

Recently I was consulted by a young chap who certainly had nothing to brag about in the way of physical attractions. To begin with he was rather less than average height, and was of the flat-chested, round-shouldered variety. Now from my point of view he was at least twenty-five pounds lighter than he should have been. Evidently he placed a high value on his personal appearance, for he dressed in a way to emphasize what points he had. A good tailor had cut his clothes, and the back of the coat was well-shaped, and in order to make him appear broad-shouldered it was tapered into the waist line and tightly belted. The trousers were rather full at the top of the legs in a way that made it seem as though he had some thigh development; and like many other flat-chested men he had a trick of buttoning only the bottom button of his coat. That made his coat flare open at the top, and thus gave the impression that there was a real chest inside of the coat.

While he was talking to me I noticed that he was looking over me in a disapproving way and he stared so earnestly at my neck that I wondered whether my collar was soiled, or my necktie disarranged. Finally he blurted out, "Mr. Liederman, I *do* want to get stronger and to have a better figure. But if you take me in hand and train me I want you to promise that you will not make me too big. Now, I wouldn't want to be as broad as you are, and particularly I wouldn't care to have a neck like yours." "Why, what's the matter with my neck?" "Oh," he said, "it is *too big*. It looks like a wrestler's neck. I don't want to be built like a wrestler or a Hercules. I want to be slim and have a good shape at the same time. I think that if a man has a thick neck and thick wrists

he looks coarse, and would be out of place in a fashionable drawing room. You know, Mr. Liederman, the
fashionable trend is toward slenderness—to keep your
boyish figure. The women like a slender, well-made man,
but these big truck-horses of men disgust them." Seeing
that I am fairly tall and weigh only about 175 pounds I
was rather surprised that I should be considered mon-
strously large, but I controlled myself and said: "Man,
I have no intention of giving you what you call a 'truck
horse build,' but if I am to give you a real build it will be
necessary to make your chest several inches bigger. That
means that the upper part of your back will be broader
and that your sides will taper in finely from your arm-
pits to the sides of your waist. Also your chest will get
rounded out and full in front, so that when viewed from
the side your chest will be thicker from front to back
than your waist is. And at present, as you must realize,
you are very little bigger around the chest than you are
around the waist. Of course, your neck will get bigger
as your chest gets bigger and your shoulders will get
broader. You would look odd if you got a bigger chest
and still had that slender neck. When I am through
with you, you may have to wear a 15½-inch collar instead of that 13½ size you now have on. However, your
neck will not look extra big, but in proportion to the rest
of you."

It was no use! My neck had scared him off—which
was a rather odd experience for me, as I had worked
hard to develop my neck to its present size and shape. If
I had talked all day I could not have made an impression
on that man's mind. I felt just like a shoemaker does,
when, after measuring a fat lady's foot and producing
the right size shoe—five C—she insists that he does not
know his business, and that in all her life she has *never*

ARTHUR SAXON

This remarkable lifter performed this stunt when with the circus. The total weight of his two brothers shown above was well over 300 pounds. He had no difficulty in bent-pressing them, one arm overhead, daily.

worn anything larger than a 2 double A; and if he cannot fit her there are other shoemakers, etc., etc.

Fashions and tastes change from year to year, but the ideal human figure does not. A beautifully made Greek athlete of 600 B.C. would be a beautifully made man of today. Conversely, a modern man, who wishes to make his body perfectly proportioned and supremely strong and enduring, cannot do better than to try and equal the proportions of some statue of Apollo, of Mercury, Theseus, Perseus, or one of the other old Greek heroes. There were well-built men before the time of the Greeks and there have been others since—even today.

I remember that when I was a boy the fashion in men's clothes was for the shoulders to be padded. Every man, in that year, who bought a new suit, immediately looked impossibly broad-shouldered. Sometimes there were pads as big as flat-irons where there should have been deltoid muscles. There was a great deal of talk about the "impressiveness of broad shoulders," and the "manly appearance of the new style." And since, like all boys, I aped my elders, I longed for the time when I could have one of those padded coats, and would be able to flaunt my (artificial) shoulders in the eyes of all beholders. Imagine my disgust when a couple of years later, I tried to get a coat of that variety, and the tailor said, "Oh! We are not padding the shoulders this year. The natural sloping shoulder is the thing."

A really well-made man does not have to depend on the cut of his clothes to give the impression of shapeliness. If he has the shape, the natural lines of his figure will set off *any* of the changing styles. This may sound more like a fashion-talk than a discussion of "the secrets of strength," but really it is important; because strength depends, as I hope to convince you, on the proportions of the body and on the size and quality of the muscles.

My hardest work is to convince a certain class of people that in order to become stronger and in general *more vital*, it is necessary to make themselves bigger. A man will tell me that he is tired of being a weakling, and would like to double or even triple his strength, if I can guarantee to do it in, say, six months. If, in reply, I say "Well, you have a good chance. I believe I can put six inches more around your chest, increase that 13-inch arm until it measures 15 inches, and give you a real pair of legs," he is apt to reply, "Oh! I don't want so much to be bigger, as to be *stronger*." I can realize that if a rather tall man of thirty, has for ten years been wearing a 36 coat, it is somewhat of a shock to realize that in a few months he will have to be wearing a size 42; but when I show that man pictures of beautifully shaped modern athletes of his height, whose bodies have beautifully smooth lines, betokening both strength and agility; and tell him that their chests measure even more than 42 inches, he realizes that a large chest is necessary, and when it begins to dawn on him that instead of having to be apologetic about his slender arms, he will get an arm like a Dempsey or Sandow, he sees that after all there is some connection between vigor and proportions.

I suppose that a watchmaker gets used to the fact that a business man will carry a watch in his pocket for a lifetime without having the least idea of how the watch works. But *I* cannot see how some young men, especially those interested in athletics, can live with their own bodies, and have so little knowledge of what their bodies should look like, and can be made to look like.

I found a young friend reading a book and he said, "Here is something that ought to interest you." I looked at the book, which told about Rajah Brooke's invasion

of Borneo; and in the paragraph it stated, "His crew
were sturdy English fighting sailors—powerful men—
not one of whom had less than a 14½-inch biceps." My
friend said, "Say Earle, is that a big arm?" I told him it
was bigger than the average; such an arm as a blacksmith, a heavy weight-lifter or prizefighter might have—
and that a 14½ biceps which might look very impressive
on a short man, would seem inadequate on a very tall and
broad-shouldered man, but nevertheless was a considerably bigger arm than the average man carried in his
sleeve. Then, "Well, what *is* a really big arm," and I
said, "Oh, sixteen to seventeen and a half inches according to the man's height."

Next, "How much does *your* arm measure?" I told
him, and countered with "And how about yours?" That
struck home. He did not know his upper arm measurement, although he did know the measurement of his
chest and waist because he ordered his own clothes; and
he knew the size shoe and collar he wore. I suppose those
things, together, with his height and weight, are as much
as the average young fellow knows about his own body.
But that the chest must be so many inches larger than
the waist in order to give the proper taper to the body;
that the chest itself must be of a certain size to insure
proper lung capacity, and that a certain size arm should
go with a certain size chest, is something of which even
the athletically inclined are usually ignorant.

So when a man asks me to make him very much
stronger without making him any bigger, I have to explain that I have no secret receptacle from which I can
take a quantity of strength and pour it into his body.
And even if I had, how could I put, say, a quart of
strength into a vessel built to hold only a pint?

To put it in another way—you can't get eighty horse-

power out of an engine which is built to develop only 40
H.P., no matter how much gas you feed into it. Even
though it is true that it is the gas that makes the engine
go, yet as a general rule the more the horse-power the
bigger and finer the engine. And you simply cannot
carry a five-ton load on a chassis built to carry 1½ tons
as the limit.

There are "Strong Men" galore, and I defy you to
bring me *one* who is either small, or weak looking. Oh!
I know there are people—men and women both—who
call themselves "Human Magnets"; who are frail in
build, and who *seem* to do great feats of strength. But if
you knew as much as I do about the show business, you
would realize that these people's strength is literally an
illusion.

Well then—among strong men we find chaps with 48-
inch chests, with 17-inch arms, and 25-inch thighs. Some
of them are lazy, and have allowed themselves to get fat
and "beefy looking." But you can rest assured that, if
they are the genuine article, underneath the fat you
can see, there are hidden steel-like muscles. Most of
them, however, "look the part"; and take pride in so
doing. Their broad shoulders, deep chests, wide backs
and muscular arms and legs all fit into the picture. And
some of the biggest of them look amazingly slender. That
is because they are big and strong in the right places.
They have the size and development that gives enormous
strength, and yet you can tell by looking at them, that
they have not sacrificed one bit of their agility; nor does
their imposing size make them clumsy. Because their development is rightly placed, it accentuates the beautiful
lines of the figure. Positively one can become strong and
powerfully built without making oneself, either very
heavy, or in the least clumsy. I know two men of exactly

the same height, one of whom is a professional "Strong Man" and the other is his manager. Both are big. Each is five feet, nine inches tall; but the manager has only a 40-inch chest and 14-inch arms; and is fat and has a 44-inch waist and weighs 220 pounds. While the athlete, who has a 44-inch chest, 16-inch arms, and a 32-inch waist, weighs 180 pounds. His hips are smaller because they carry no fat, but his legs are as big, far better shaped, and *infinitely stronger* than those of his manager. And he weighs forty pounds less, although he is a bigger framed man. True, he carries no fat except that small quantity which every healthy human being has to have. The bones of the two men are about the same size. If you could in any way segregate the pure muscular fiber of the fat manager, you would find that his actual muscles were only about half the size of the strong man's. All of which seems to prove that healthy well-trained muscular fiber weighs less than fat. It would be interesting to know just how much soft, useless fat a stout man carries around the middle of his body.

It is my experience that a man who is naturally slender, can so develop his body that it will be almost perfectly shaped; can increase his strength twofold or threefold, without the slightest danger of putting himself in the "truck-horse" class.

Let us take as an example, the average young fellow, say 23 or 24 years old. The likelihood is that he will stand about 5 feet 7½ inches in height (for that is the average height), will weigh between 135 or 140 pounds clothed; and that he will take a "size 36" coat and a 14½ collar. Now, if we make that man strip for a physical examination, we will find that by shedding his clothes his weight comes down close to 130 pounds. That removing his shoes has reduced his height to 5 feet 7 inches, or

THOMAS INCH

The famous English strong man, who created some remarkable records as a middle-weight lifter. It is said that Mr. Inch, just to win a wager, in a very short time converted his body from a middle-weight into a heavy-weight without losing any of his splendid proportions.

less. And his chest which he fondly imagines measures 36 inches *because his coat is that size, actually* measures between 34 and 35 inches. If you attire him in a pair of trunks and take his photograph, he is apt to be surprised and dismayed when he sees the picture. "Why" he will say "I had no idea I was so skinny as that. I look as though I could stand 20 pounds more weight." And it would be easy for him to put on that much weight simply by developing his muscles through the right kind of exercise.

The picture shows that he has just about as little muscular tissue as will enable his body and limbs to function. His back is about the same width all the way from shoulders to hips; almost without shape at all, and decidedly without that magnificent taper from arm-pits to waist that is shown by the really strong. The front of his body is perfectly smooth. His collar-bones which should be completely hidden, stick out like two rails. There is hardly an indication of the big muscles that should cover the chest, and his abdomen is as smooth and muscleless as that of a ten-year-old boy. Because he has always worn stiff collars, his neck is thin and pokes forward. His shoulder-blades protrude a bit. His arms measure perhaps about ten inches just below the elbow, and even less than that above the elbow, when the arms are hanging at the sides. His legs, which he has had to use in walking, are better than the rest of him; but the chances are that around the calves he measures not more than 13½ inches, and that his thighs, even at the biggest part, measure 20 inches or less. Assuming that his work has been of a sedentary character, it is no wonder that his physique is so poor. The muscles grow by use, and the indoor workers—office men, clerks, students, and the like—hardly use their muscles at all. They are in the habit of riding even if they have only a few blocks to go; and during the day the hardest work they do is to pick up a ledger or move some light packages.

Put such a fellow as I have described on a farm and you will almost see him grow from week-end to week-end. Because he is continually moving about—stooping, lifting, carrying, hoeing and pitching hay—he has to use almost all his muscles. His back will become thicker and broader; his shoulders will straighten up and get square in outline. His chest will be bigger. His legs in particular will get more sturdy and his arms will have a capable, sinewy look. In ten weeks of such outdoor work a young man will gain 20 pounds in weight; practically all of which is good solid muscle tissue. Naturally his eating has had something to do with it. Being continually in the open air in itself promotes appetite; but using his muscles ten hours a day is the real factor. For all that time he is putting forth energy and he will have to eat very much more in order to *keep up his strength*, than he did when working indoors. He sleeps soundly because he is healthily tired; he eats all he can get, and he is using his muscles practically all the time; *and muscles grow from use*. His gain in weight is due entirely to something new that he has created for himself—bigger muscles for the harder work.

You may tell me that all this is nothing new; that "Anybody knows *that*." When you go on a vacation and play games, or when you take a job at laboring, you *expect* to build up, and put on flesh if you are thin; and to reduce weight if you are fat. That you think, is the regular and natural thing.

Well, then, let us look at it from another angle. Grant that, at the end of your ten weeks on the farm, you *are* a huskier physical specimen than when you started in. You look better, you feel better, and you know you *are* better. You can carry a heavy sack of potatoes that you could not have even lifted on the first day; you can keep on for hours at back-breaking labor that would have crippled you in the old days. You have a grand feeling of hardiness and capability. (And all of that is the result of *un*systematic work, that is, unsystematic *muscular* work. For farm labor, while it calls heavily on certain muscles, leaves others almost untouched.) When you look at yourself in a mirror, you seem to be bigger all around than previously; but except in a few places there are but few indications of any pronounced increase in the size and shape of the muscles. Your back is infinitely better, for you have somehow acquired two big cables of muscle along each side of the spine, and there seems to be two or three times as much muscle across your shoulder blades as before. The points of your shoulders are much rounder. Your forearms are perhaps an inch bigger, your hands bigger and harder, and even your wrists seem thicker. Your thighs while not so very much bigger, are *rounder* than formerly, and look bigger when you view them from the side. All that is gratifying, but you are somewhat puzzled by the fact that your upper arms have not become as big and round and heavily muscled as the rest of you. You have developed but little muscle on the front of the body itself (breast and abdomen) and the front and sides of the thighs have not assumed those big, swelling, and impressive curves you are accustomed to see on the legs of track athletes, football players and tumblers.

But that you have gained at all is gratifying, and you feel if you could afford it you would always do several hours' muscular work every day. If you did, you would in all probability be disappointed in the results. For after a very few months of *daily* hard labor you would find that the body would lose its power to *more than renew itself.* That the work instead of steadily increasing your size and strength, would tend to tire you; that your energy would gradually be drained, and that instead of having a surplus you would have a deficit.

Laboring men and farmers are undoubtedly, *as a class*, stronger than indoor workers; but also, as a class, they are not very strong. No laborer uses his back more than a coal-heaver, yet the average oarsman who rows only a hundred hours in the whole year, is apt to have a stronger back than the average coal-heaver. Similarly a gymnast who uses his arm muscle only an hour a day will have a stronger arm than the average blacksmith who uses his arm eight times as much. I can use this undoubted fact to prove to you that it takes very much less time and trouble to develop a strong body than it does to properly train your mind, and that systematic exercise produces more strength than does hard labor.

Because I have always been interested in muscular development, I am a close observer of the effects of different kinds of exercise, and different schemes of training. And always I have found that methodical, systematic *exercise* produces vastly greater results in muscle making and strength building than does, hit-or-miss unsystematic *work.*

We have seen how a slender young fellow can add considerably to his bodily weight and muscular strength by getting outdoors and doing actual labor. As far as general improvement is concerned, he can get just about as much net results by working in a gymnasium for an hour each evening, during ten successive weeks. I say "working" advisedly; because I believe that it is impossible to get a high degree of either muscle, or strength, unless you *work* for it. If you join a "gymnasium class" and spend the whole session in performing elementary drills, such as waving the arms, and gently bending the body this way and that, you will, to be sure, *awaken* your muscular system and improve your circulation, but you will not gain perceptibly in development; nor will you become very much stronger. If, however, you go to a "gym" which is not given up entirely to "class-work," which is patronized by men who like "real exercise," and where you have the unrestricted use of all the apparatus, you can increase the size and strength of your muscles just as much or more, than you can by outdoor labor.

Suppose after a week or two spent at doing easy stunts, your muscles commence to harden up, and you attempt the more vigorous stunts that give them harder and harder work. At the end of the month or so when you go to the gym, instead of spending the hour doing mild calisthenics your program is something like this: You get on the flying rings and do a few stunts to limber yourself up. You practice a bit at bar-vaulting, raising the bar after each vault. You join some of the other members and practice some tumbling and hand-balancing stunts. You do some rope climbing, "chinning the bar," "dipping" on the parallels; pull away vigorously for a few minutes on the rowing-machine; use the springboard for your legs and the "rack" for your abdominal and side muscles; and maybe wind up the evening at a bout of wrestling with some active opponent.

Under such a program you can, and *will* build up rapidly. Just as rapidly as though you spent *all* your waking hours at *labor*. You exercise pretty much all of your muscles, and because you do things which require strength, you create the strength with which to do them. And at the end of a few weeks you will find that you

ANTONE MATYSEK

A famous strong man, who is an artist with dumb-bells. His abundance of nervous energy, perfect balance and exceptionally well-trained muscles make him a past master in lifting.

have outgrown your clothes, and that your friends are remarking at your improved appearance.

The effects of this kind of gym work are more visible than the effects of farm work, and also of a different character. While work on the farm provides active exercise, and increased strength in the back, the shoulders, the forearms and part of the legs; the gym work tends to give less work to those parts and more to the upper arms, the chest, and abdominal and side muscles, and to other, and different muscles on the legs. Moreover, gym work makes you springier and more active than does farm labor, produces almost as good an appetite and certainly makes your muscles stand out more prominently.

But even then, such unsystematic gym practice does not create great strength; all it does is to make you as strong as the others who use the gym. And while the average all-round gymnast is stronger than the average farmer, or day laborer, and *very* much stronger and better developed than the average man; yet he falls far short of being as strong as those men who have deliberately trained with the idea of becoming as strong and as well-shaped as is possible for a man to be.

In the course of a day's work the farm-hand may have to exert the full strength of his back muscles only once or twice. In the course of an evening's workout, the gymnast may do many things which require a full and powerful contraction of his muscles. Which explains why the gymnasts' arm muscles, for instance, are bigger, better-developed, and more powerful than those of the farm-hand. It is a truism to say that the strongest muscle is the one which can contract against the greatest resistance; but it is not generally known that the contractile strength of a muscle can be purposely and definitely increased by training it to contract against an ever-in-

creasing resistance. The same power can be developed
by causing the muscles to make what is known as a "full
contraction" instead of the partial contraction which is
all that is required when working or doing gymnastic
stunts.

Anyone who has spent much of his time around gymnasiums is familiar with the remarkable development
that comes from specializing in certain kinds of vigorous
work, and the incredible strength which comes from such
development. I was only a kid when I first joined a gym,
and more by good luck than by good management, I
happened to pick out one that was patronized by a lot of
professional athletes, gymnasts and stage performers.
Everything, in fact, from contortionists to circus
"Strong Men."

Each of these men was in his way a specialist who
earned his living by his trained muscles; and since I
associated with them daily and watched them train, I
naturally learned a lot.

I would watch a jumper training his thigh muscles
and a gymnast coaxing up his arm strength. I recall
there were two men in that crowd who particularly
aroused my enthusiasm. One of them was a "Roman
Ring Artist" who was at that time a great drawing-card
in the big vaudeville circuits. The extraordinary thing
about him was his arm and shoulder development. Up to
then I had never seen such arms. I never thought to ask
him how much they measured, but I suppose they must
have spanned close to 17 inches. Even when he walked
around, just swinging his arms naturally, the biceps and
triceps muscles between the elbow and shoulder would
ripple and roll under the skin in a way that fascinated
me. And his shoulders! Well, he was not particularly
broad, but covering the points of the shoulders were del-

toid muscles literally as big as cocoanuts. His breast-muscles were as big as any I have ever seen, and his back seemed like a mass of interwoven straps, and ropes of muscle.

Every day when he came in for practice, he would walk over to the rings, pull himself up very slowly, shift his weight from one hand to the other, curl with one hand at a time, do "Planches" and other revolutions; but always very, very slowly.

When I asked him why he always started off with these slow movements, he told me that it was because it was much harder to do the things slowly, and required more strength. That he had to have a lot of strength, for that when he did his stuff before an audience it was necessary to do the hardest tricks as though they were easy to him. He also explained to me the necessity of fully flexing the muscles and told me how he had "worked up" his strength. Like most specialists he had an uneven development. He had the torso and arms of a Hercules, and the legs and hips of a non-athlete. See him only from the waist up and you would guess that he weighed 180 pounds. See only his legs and he looked like a 125-pounder. So he must originally have had a small frame, and it would be interesting to know whether he could have developed legs equally as good as his arms if he had trained his leg muscles as thoroughly as he had his arms. Then he was very strong in certain ways but not in others. He could tear three packs of cards, and it was a cinch for him to twist iron bars in the way that at present seems so wonderful to some of you. I doubt though, whether he could have lifted a very heavy weight off the ground, simply because he didn't have the legs for that kind of stunt; and I imagine that he could not have carried 500 pounds on one shoulder the way that some

"Strong Men" carry twice that much. Because, in the first place, the muscles at the sides of his waist were not strong enough to keep him from doubling over sideways, and in the second place his legs were so frail that they would have buckled at the knees at the first step. Undoubtedly he was a strong-armed man, but whether he was a "Strong Man" is a question, for no man is really strong unless he is strong all over.

Another man in that gym, who interested me, was an old gentleman who was one of the few amateurs who frequented the place. I did not know his exact age, but from things he said I judged that he was a boy in Civil War days, and must have become interested in exercise in the 1870's; a time at which there was a vogue for a device called a "health-lift." All he was interested in was lifting weights off the floor; and he had made a contraption on which he could load a 100-pound weight and at the top of the affair was a handle, or cross-bar, which reached up about twenty-eight inches. This man had the theory that if every day you thoroughly exercised your back muscles, you would keep your figure, your health, and your strength into advanced old age. So every afternoon he would drop in and have a short session with his lifting-machine. He would pile on three or four hundred pounds, stand with straight legs, bend his body by arching his spine a trifle, and lift the weight by straightening his back. He would put on more weights and practice what professionals call the "hand-and-thigh" lift. He would keep his back straight and bend his legs at the knees, grasp the handle-bar, so that his knuckles would rest against the front of the thigh; and lift the weight by straightening the legs and heaving up the shoulders. After two or three repetitions he would pile on more weight, and it was customary to work up to 1,000 or 1,200 pounds before he quit. On one occasion to settle an argument he lifted 1,500 pounds dead weight in the "hand-and-thigh style." I cannot tell you how long he had exercised in that way, but he must have been at it forty years when I knew him. And as he rarely missed a day, there was very good reason for his profound faith in his own method of keeping himself strong and healthy. As a result of his specialized work he had a most peculiar development. His thighs, both back and front, were unusually big and his calves were enormous. Naturally he had big chains of muscles along the spine, but the striking thing was the phenomenal development of the trapezius muscles, which are in the upper back just below the base of the neck. These muscles, when they contract, "shrug up" the shoulders, and when he did his "hand-and-thigh" lift and heaved his shoulders up, you could see these muscles bunch themselves into two enormous masses. Even when standing at ease these muscles were so big that they made his shoulders slope at a high angle up from the deltoids to the sides of his neck. No ready-made coat would fit him. His forearms—especially the outside parts of them —were covered with muscles so powerfully developed that there were big furrows between them. His grip was something to be avoided. His biceps muscles were pronounced in their size, but his whole upper arm was small compared to his forearm; and notwithstanding his ability to lift enormous weights from the ground he could not lift big dumb-bells over head.

My objections to his plan were, that by giving *very* heavy work to only a few sets of muscles he had made those muscles stiff and rather slow in action; and by his specialization he had failed both to realize the full

JOHN Y. SMITH

The famous lifter who was a master at the bent press. Perhaps not as massively
proportioned as some famous strong men, yet he knew all the secrets of strength
which I have endeavored to unfold within these pages.

strength of his whole body and had spoiled the symmetry of that body.

I was particularly interested in the effects of his exercise. So far as I could see, his heart was perfectly sound
and strong, and as an explanation he told me that he
never lifted so much that it made him red in the face.
The moment he felt that there was a strain on the blood-
vessels, he would stop and lighten the weight. You might
think that his constant dead-weight lifting would have
broken down the arches in his feet, but the exact opposite was the case, for the work which developed the big
muscles in his calves seemed to give equal strength to the
muscles of the feet.

Then there was the man who used nothing but pulley-
weights. Nowadays the pulley-weights you find in gymnasiums are small things, equipped with a few weights of
a pound apiece. But this one was a massive affair with
thick cords and provided with ten weights of five pounds
each. So, if you cared to, you could put 25 pounds on
the end of each pulley. This enthusiast never stood up
when exercising, because, he said, when you stood on
your feet you unconsciously used your body weight to
help in the work. So he would sit on a stool facing the
pulley weights; and would go through a lot of movements very slowly and steadily. Then he would reverse,
and sit with his back to the machine and do a lot more. I
have seen him work for thirty minutes without stopping
and at the end of that time the surrounding floor would
be wet with his sweat. Certainly he had a wonderful development from the diaphragm upwards, but below the
level of his lowest ribs he was only average.

In those days they cared for nothing except big arm,
shoulder and upper-body development. If they had their
pictures taken they knew but one pose, and that was to

sit in a chair with their arms folded across the chest and the biceps muscles pushed out by the hidden fingers.

There was a man who pinned all his faith to the "upright parallels"—a pair of bars set perpendicular to the floor instead of horizontal. The thing was to stand between these bars, grasp one in each hand at the height of your nipples, and then to lunge the body forwards and backwards. According to this man that was the only exercise anyone needed. "For," he said, "when you throw your weight backwards you develop all the muscles on the rear half of your body, and also strengthen your back, and when you lunge forward and through the bars, you open up the chest and develop all the muscles on the front of your body. If you don't believe it look at me." And that would end the argument, for when you looked him over you could not but admit the beauty of his build. None of his muscles were very big, but they were all good-sized. His chest was roomy and he had, I think, the widest back I have ever seen on a man of his height. The general lines of his figure were grand. He gave credit to the upright parallels for all his development—even for his fine legs. It happened that three or four times a week he would play handball for one hour, and he apparently forgot that *that* was what developed his legs—for the upright parallels positively will not make the legs either much bigger or much stronger.

Looking back I can see where I must have been an awful nuisance to some of those men, for I was continually pestering them with questions and trying to drag information out of them. I fear I have always been that way. If I saw a man with amazing muscles in his chest I would have to know what he did to develop them. If a man had large and wonderfully shaped thighs I would ask him how they got that way; and whether the legs just grew that way, or whether he had succeeded in giving them their size and shape by exercising; and if so, what exercises did he favor. I was a "bear" on measurements and would embarrass these athletes by demanding to know exactly how much—to a fraction of an inch—their arms, legs and chests measured.

I may have been over-zealous, but I sure learned a lot. I found that the better a man was, the more willing he was to help you. After all, the secrets of acquiring strength are: first, to know what to do, and second, to do it. So these wise old birds had no hesitation in telling me just how to improve my development, and increase my strength, because they knew very well that it would not help me unless I had the ambition to become *strong and the willingness to work* to get strong. Today people consider that I am exceptionally well developed—all I can say is that I deserve to be, because I certainly worked for it.

Chapter IV

Are Small Bones a Bar to Strength?

AMONG those interested in muscle-culture, there is a widespread, but I believe erroneous, belief that only those who have big bones can get a fine muscular development. That is an idea which should be combated, because, as a fact, beauty of form (that is, perfect proportions), pronounced muscular development and great strength *can* be acquired by any man, be his bones large or small, if he cares enough for such things to work to get them.

Let us start out by acknowledging that there is a basis for the belief that big bones make for big muscles. More of us feel that instinctively, when we see a big gawky boy of sixteen or seventeen, perhaps six feet tall, rather broad-shouldered and with noticeably large hands and feet. His extremities seem big, because the rest of his body is not particularly large, and that makes his hands big by comparison. Almost invariably we think "that chap is going to be a big man some day when he grows up to his hands and feet." In other words we recognize that the boy has the frame, but has not yet had time to "fill out." A man may be tall because his bones are longer than the average, but it takes more than mere length of bone to give size to the extremities.

A big-handed man or boy usually has thick wrists, broad palms, big joints and rather thick fingers. In a big-footed individual the foot is broad as well as long— and of course big bones make big joints. Most of the bones in the arms and legs are long with a knob at each end, the shape of the knob depending on the individual bone. It is hardly necessary to explain that the size of

87

the knobs, say of the upper arm bone, bears a certain proportion to the thickness of the shaft of the bones; that is, a thick bone will have larger knobs at each end than will a thin bone. Therefore a man whose upper-arm bones are thick, and whose neighboring bones are correspondingly thick, will have bigger elbow and shoulder joints than will a man whose upper arm-bones are slender and where the knobs or the ends of the bones are small in proportion to the slender shaft. All that sounds dry and technical but it is something you must learn.

As all of you studied physiology in school you know that a muscle tapers off into tendons, and that these tendons are attached to the bones. Sometimes the tendons are round like cords, sometimes flat like ribbons, and in other cases the tendinous attachment is broad. Sometimes the tendons are attached at the ends of the bones near the knob and sometimes to grooves in the bones. The part I am trying to make clear is this: Since there are certain places or spaces to which the tendons are attached, it stands to reason that on a big bone those places are bigger than on a small bone. Therefore, it is equally reasonable to say that the bigger the bone the bigger the tendons. And following that up, the bigger the tendons the bigger the muscles that rise from (or taper into) those tendons.

That is one way to state the case, and when so stated it does seem kind of hopeless for a man with slender and delicately made bones to try and get the rugged development which a man who has thick bones seems to acquire without particular effort. It is my opinion that people believe these things without being able to explain them. Certainly almost any man, young or old, will argue on those lines if you can get him to discuss his chances of becoming strong and muscular. It has gotten so that a

LOUIS CYR
The giant Canadian record holder, whose colossal
proportions and immense strength seemed almost
unbelievable.

man will tell you that he is naturally of the "truck-horse type," or "the race-horse type"; and will scout at the idea that his type is in any way changeable. Well, perhaps so, and perhaps not. But don't forget that, after all, it *is* possible through exercise to enlarge and to change the shape of the body, or belly, of the muscle, whether it is equipped at its termination with either stout or thin tendons. A young fellow may suddenly become dissatisfied with the size and shape of his upper arms. It may be a day in April that he notices how thin they are. Having planned to spend part of August at the seashore, he vows that by then he will have a decent-looking pair of arms.

He looks at his wrists, and says, "Huh! Not much bigger than a girl's." He examines his upper arm, puts a tape around it and finds that the reading is all of eleven inches. Doubles up his arm and looks at it in the mirror. Instead of showing a big lump of biceps, as it should, the shape of the arm is hardly different from when he holds it straight. There is a long low curve that shows where the biceps is, and that is all. On the back of the arm there is no indication of muscle. But he knows the muscles are there, for after all he can move his arms around the same as other folks can. He understands that the problem is to make those muscles bigger, and to get control of them so that they will stand out in pleasing curves.

So every morning he exercises with, say, a pair of 5-pound dumb-bells, and in the evenings he practices "chinning the bar" for his biceps muscles, and "dipping" on the floor for the triceps of his arms. At first he can "chin" himself only once or twice, and "dip" three or four times. But he is a "plugger" and by the time midsummer comes around he can chin himself fifteen or twenty times without much trouble, and performs thirty or forty "dips" in succession. His arm muscles have responded to the regular hard work and the tape—which at first showed only 11 inches—now registers 13½ inches when he passes it around his flexed biceps muscle.

A 13½-inch arm is very far from being wonderful, but it looks so good in comparison to what it looked like in April that the young man takes great pride in it, and instead of dreading the ordeal of appearing in a sleeveless jersey, he anticipates flattering remarks about the size and shape of his arms. To increase the size of the upper arm by 2½ inches in four months, is nothing at all remarkable, particularly when the arm was very thin to start with. If the arm had measured 13½ inches at the start and had been increased to 16 inches it would have been much more noteworthy. But even *that* is possible and I have seen it happen, in the case of one of these tall, big-framed, broad-shouldered men; and while in his undeveloped stage a 13½-inch arm looked as thin on him as an 11-inch arm does on a small-boned man of short stature.

Once I was discussing with a noted "Strong Man" the increase in strength that comes from graded weight-lifting. I mentioned a young man who had apparently tripled his lifting power in six months' training. "Yes," said my friend, "but that is about as far as he will go. I know him and I can tell you that he has realized all the strength that was in him. Look at his frame! It will not stand much more muscle. If he keeps on practicing he may improve his records by becoming more skilful, but I very much doubt whether he will get any bigger or actually any stronger."

This was a professional, who sincerely believes that there are limitations imposed by nature. There are other professionals (I am one of them) who believe that it is possible in some ways to overcome the handicaps of small bones and a naturally delicate physique.

Let us consider the arms, because they create most interest in the beginners. The small-boned man starts out by saying "it is impossible for *me* to get a big arm on account of my wrists being so very slender." He does not say whether he refers to the whole arm, to the forearm or the upper arm. In the forearm there are two bones, and their lower ends, which lie side by side, form part of the wrist-joint. The two forearm bones run roughly parallel to each other, and the placement of the bones governs in some measure the size of the forearm. That is, if the bones are close together, the forearm will be narrow when you hold the arm out in front of you with palm up. If there is a greater space between the bones, then the forearm will be broad. Since the longer of the two bones has a very considerable knob at its lower end, it can be readily seen that in an arm where the bones are big and thick, the extra size of the knob will *tend* to set the bones further apart, thus making the wrist bigger and the forearm broader. Small bones may place a definite limit on the extent to which the forearms can be developed but the same thing is less true of the upper arm.

In the upper arm there is only one bone, and the thickness of that bone is small when compared to the thickness of the arm itself. In the upper arm there is far more muscle-contents than bone-contents; and in the forearm it should be noted that there is more muscle at its upper end where the bones are close together.

The fact that it is hard for some men to develop big forearms (even by the hardest kind of work) positively does not make it impossible for them to develop big and wonderfully muscled upper arms.

One authority on the subject, who to say the least, is a man of very wide experience, says that the best most men can do in this way of development is to get a forearm 1 9-10 times the size of the wrist and that the *flexed* upper arm should measure 1-5 more than the forearm. To quote his own example: a man with a seven-inch wrist can get a 13 3-10-inch forearm and a 16-inch upper arm. He does not claim that this is the limit, but does claim that such proportions are possible to *any* man who will exercise hard enough.

Thirteen-inch forearms are comparatively rare, even in big men; and then you usually find them terminating in a wrist which is $7\frac{1}{4}$ or $7\frac{1}{2}$ inches around.

While I believe that the figures given by the authority just mentioned are possible, and that perhaps they show ideal proportions, my experience is that the forearm is apt to be smaller in proportion to the wrist, and that the upper arm can be developed until it is more than 25 per cent. bigger than the forearm.

There is a "Strong Man" who was quite prominent a few years ago who, to my positive knowledge, has a $7\frac{1}{4}$-inch wrist, a $12\frac{1}{2}$-inch forearm and a $16\frac{1}{2}$-inch upper arm. His wrists are bony-looking, his forearms are terrifically strong, despite their comparatively small size, and his upper arms are wonderful. Figure out his proportions and you will find that his forearm is only a little more than 1 7-10 times the size of his wrist and that his upperarm, instead of being only 20 per cent. larger than the forearm, is actually 33 per cent., or about one-third larger. And if that man could have developed his forearms any more he would have done so, because he was justifiably proud of his strength and his development, and would go to any trouble to improve himself in either respect.

I adduce this case to prove two things. First, that big wrists do not necessarily imply big forearms; and second, that the size of the upper arm is not limited by the size of the forearm.

If you were to examine a lot of ditch-diggers, or lumber-choppers, or any other class of men who use their arms continually, you would find that as a rule their forearms are large in proportion to the upper arms. While in gymnasts, "Strong Men" tumblers, and physical culturists in general, you would find the opposite to be the case; that the upper arms were unusually big as compared to the forearms. I myself, who have an upper arm measuring $16\frac{1}{2}$ inches, am a case in point; for I have never been able to get my forearm up to quite 13 inches, this leaving my upper arm over 25 per cent. larger than my forearm; and my wrist is hardly seven inches around. I admit that it is an advantage, from the standpoint of strength, to have big bones on which to build, but I refuse to admit that big bones are essential—or that a small-boned man is *doomed* to have small muscles.

There are those who think that shortness of stature— lack of height— is a positive bar to strength or development, and it is particularly hard to persuade them that any man can become possessed of great strength no matter what his height.

In the course of your life you have probably seen a number of professional "Strong Men" performing in circuses, or on the vaudeville stage. In addition it is likely that you have seen some amateur athletes of great strength, and perhaps there are among your own friends one or two men who are exceedingly strong.

If you were asked to describe a "Strong Man," you would undoubtedly say that such a man was strongly built, with fine shoulders, big chest, powerful legs and

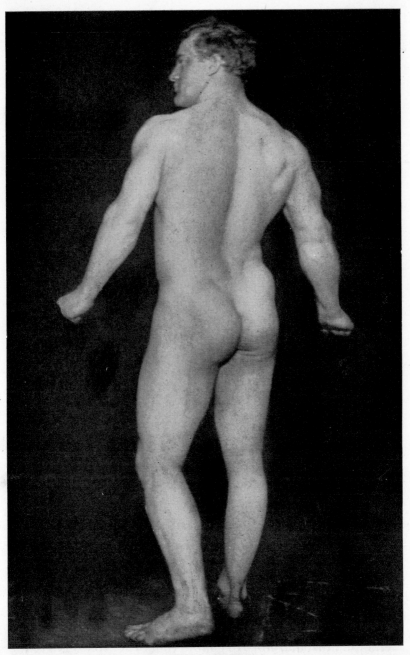

ADOLPH NORDQUEST

A striking pose of this famous strong man. While a trifle taller than his brother, Joseph, his Herculean proportions are more evenly distributed. This photograph portrays a most interesting display of the back of Adolph Nordquest. In this photograph can be seen how perfectly each muscle blends with the other. Adolph is noted for his strong back. His every posture suggests strength.

tremendously muscled arms. Also, if you were speaking of a professional, you would mention that his muscles were not only big but were very "clean-cut" and well-shaped.

I would be willing to wager that you have never seen a real "Strong Man" who was either very thin or who showed no muscle. The very idea of strength is connected in your mind with individuals of a certain bulk or a certain development. For my part, and remember that I have known scores of them, I have never known a "Strong Man" who had an arm smaller than 14 inches around. Nor have I known any man capable of feats of great strength who had a chest smaller than 40 inches. That goes for all of them, tall and short, big and little. Some years ago I saw a great deal of the famous Frenchman, Pierre Gasnier, and Pierre was a short man, for his head came scarcely past my shoulder. He had a chest like a barrel, and big, splendidly rounded arms and shoulders—and was so strong that he could toss around a 100-pound dumb-bell as easily as you would handle a medicine ball. His bones were perhaps a little bigger than those of most men of his height, but certainly no larger than those of the average middle-sized man.

I could name for you a dozen "Strong Men," none of them who are more than 5 feet 4 inches tall; and the least developed of them has a 15-inch arm and a 42-inch chest. In fact, nature seems to impose the rule that no man can do extreme feats of strength unless he has a body and limbs of a certain size—that is girth. It appears that a chest smaller than 40 inches will not harbor enough power, and arms smaller than 14 inches do not contain enough muscular fibre to enable the owner to exert great strength. Like all other rules, this one may have exceptions, but I have never happened to come across one of those exceptions.

It certainly is odd the way Dame Nature evens things up; or better still, the way she enables *you* to even things up. Otherwise how is it that when a short man trains to become strong he will get just about as big arms and chest and develop as much, or almost as much, power as do the big chaps?

I saw a "Strong Act" where two did Herculean feats, lifting each other around in ways that bespoke immense muscular power; and holding balances that required the utmost of muscular control. One of them was 5 feet 10 inches tall and weighed 175 pounds, the other was only 5 feet 4 inches and weighed 150 pounds. Both of them measured about the same, having 42-inch chests, 15-inch arms and 23-inch thighs. True, the taller one was more gracefully built, having longer and finer lines; and the shorter one looked somewhat chunky. As far as actual strength was concerned there was little to choose between them. The big man by reason of his greater weight could show more power in certain ways, and his longer arms and legs were an advantage in some feats which involved a sling-like movement. But the smaller man, being what we call "short-coupled," could exert more strength in feats where a shorter leverage was an advantage.

And that brings me back to a subject I mentioned before: the common desire to possess the so-called "elegant" figure. Time and again, when talking to a short man, I find a positive dislike of certain types of build. A short man will express the most enthusiastic desire to become strong and especially to possess a great muscular development, and I will assess his possibilities for him, carefully explaining how, even with his slight frame, he can get a 40-inch chest and that with such a chest he is bound to get an impressive pair of shoulders. And it frequently happens that when I get that far, I will notice a far-away look in his eyes, and know that he is trying to make a mental picture of himself as he will appear when fully developed. Finally he will break out, and say "But if I had as big a chest as that and broad shoulders it would make me look squat and chunky. I don't want to look *too* heavy." And then I have to tell him that he cannot have his cake and eat it too. Everyone is entitled to his likes and dislikes, and if a man prefers slenderness to strength, no one can find fault with him. But this happens to be a book on the "secrets of strength," and it also happens that great strength entails a body of certain girth, and muscles of at least a certain size.

A large part of the population has a distinct prejudice against massiveness; and seems unable to understand that a person can be big without being massive. Given correct proportions even the most powerfully developed man can and will present a graceful appearance.

There lives in Massachusetts a 60-year-old man named Oscar Matthes. In 1884 he was famous as a "Strong Man"; in 1894 he was even more famous; and today he is still a man of great power. Here is one of the cases which proves the value of systematic exercise, for when a child he was so small and puny that exercise was prescribed as necessary. He never got over being small in one way—in height. He never was taller than 4 feet 11 inches, and when in training never weighed more than 105 pounds. And here is what he accomplished by dint of regular and systematic exercise. He got his measurements up to the following figures: Wrist $6\frac{1}{4}$ inches, forearm 12, biceps $14\frac{1}{2}$, chest 40, waist 28, hips 35, thigh 21, calf $14\frac{3}{4}$ and neck 14 inches.

There is encouragement for any man, and incidentally

there is the answer to those short people who are afraid
of becoming chunky. Too, Mr. Matthes is not chunky, but
is in all respects just a miniature Hercules. A 14½-inch
arm on a man less than five feet tall! How many *tall* men
who read this book have an arm that big? And a wrist
only 6¼ inches around! How many of my readers have
such a handicap as that? Matthes must have had very
small bones to start with, as those wrists prove. And that
he was of slender frame is shown by the comparative size
of his chest, waist and hips. A man with a 28-inch waist
simply cannot be chunky in appearance, for these
chunky men have bodies like barrels; bodies almost the
same size all the way down. Since Matthes' chest is 12
inches larger than his waist, he must have a finely taper-
ing body; and the fact that his hips are five inches smaller
than the chest helps to add an appearance of lightness to
the figure. Here we have in a small man the very spread
of shoulder, the great chest, and the trim hips that
novelists rave about.

It is interesting to note that Matthes' arms have just
about the proportions recommended by the authority already quoted. His upper arm is exactly 20 per cent.
larger than his forearm; and his forearm a trifle more
then 1 9-10 times the size of the wrist. If you take the
trouble to look again at Matthes' measurements you will
agree with me that they are not very large, except in proportion to the man's height. As already said the average
young fellow of middle height has a 35-inch chest and a
12-inch arm. Most athletes of middle height have bigger
measurements than that, and there are many gymnasts,
football players and the like, who have 40-inch chests and
14½-inch arms, and who weigh around 160 pounds. Certainly a 40-inch chest and 14½-inch arm would be
nothing out of the way for a strong man of medium

height. In Matthes' case the secret of his great strength is the marvelous muscular development of the man *compared to his height and his small frame.* If ever a man owed his strength to his development, then Matthes does. To give you an idea of that strength, I can tell you that he has a record of 10 feet 7 inches in the standing broad jump, has "chinned" himself three times with one hand, and on one occasion lifted with hands alone off an 18-inch platform, carried ten feet and then placed on another platform 24 inches high, a barrel weighing 513 pounds. If that last isn't strength, then please tell me what it is. For he had not the advantage of weighing a great deal himself, and consequently had none of the so-called power of the big men; nothing to help him but sheer strength.

While a small-boned man may have trouble in building up big forearms, and large shapely calves, he has far less difficulty in getting a fine development of the upper arms and thighs; and practically none in putting powerful, shapely muscles on the body itself. I have never found it hard to put big muscles on a pupil's chest, or his upper back, no matter how small his bones were.

I think, and most experienced trainers will agree with me, that the hardest part of the body to develop is the calf of the leg. The size of the ankle does not have as much effect on the size of the calf as does the wrist in respect to the forearm. It is true that with a 16-inch calf you will usually find a big ankle; but it is not uncommon to find a man who has big ankles and but little calf development. Also you will often find men who have slender, round ankles and incredibly developed calves. The calf of the leg is a puzzle to many trainers and the despair of many physical culturists. There are no other muscles which so obstinately refuse to grow in size and improve in

ADOLPH NORDQUEST

Another interesting pose of this famous athlete. Besides being a great lifter he is
an accomplished hand-balancer, tumbler and wrestler. His magnificent proportions can be appreciated in the above photograph.

shape, as those which lie between the ankle and the knee. It is easy to make them strong, but to change their appearance is quite another matter. I know a man who is a professional wrestler and weight-lifter, and who is unquestionably one of the most magnificently built men in the whole world—from the knees up. According to the old rules of proportion, in a well-proportioned man, the neck, the flexed upper arms and the calves of the legs should measure the same. But this man has an 18-inch neck, upper arms that measure 17½ inches (when he tenses his muscles), and calves which are only 15 inches around. Incidentally he is 5 feet 8 inches tall and weighs 215 pounds when in condition. He has thick wrists and large ankles, and while his *fore*arm measures fully 14 inches, the calves of his legs only girth one-quarter of an inch more than those of little Mr. Matthes, who has *tiny* ankles. I asked this big fellow how it was that his calves were so puny compared to the rest of him, and he frankly said that he could give no explanation. He acknowledged that he had never taken any pains to develop them, and doubted whether they would be any stronger if he did succeed in making them bigger. That his calf muscles are very strong, no one who has seen him in action could doubt; for in wrestling he can stand with firmly planted feet and toss the heaviest opponents around as though they were feather-beds. And on one occasion I saw him put a 500-pound weight on his shoulders and squat several times in succession (squatting is really a thigh exercise, but the calves have to assume part of the work), and no one with weak lower legs can squat while supporting a really heavy weight.

I have a theory about the calves, though I cannot swear that it amounts to anything. I have observed that it is the shape rather than the size of the ankle which governs the size of the calf.

If the ankle is thick from side to side, then the calf will be deep from front to back. On the contrary if the ankle is thin from side to side then, while the calf may have a fair width, it will lack that fulness in the rear part which adds so much to its size and pleasing contour. This seems somewhat contradictory, for one would think that if the ankle was thick from front to back, the calf would be likewise; whereas just the reverse is the case. This is tied up in some way with the *placement* of the ankle bones, for if the knobs of bone which appear at the sides of the ankle, are placed well forward, the calf is apt to be small, but if they are set further back the calf will be larger.

A somewhat similar condition is often noticed in the wrist, because men who have wrists of a certain shape rarely have any trouble in securing a great forearm development. Very frequently you see men whose wrists are so slender as to cause remark. There will be no sign of any bone at the thumb side of the wrist, while at the little-finger side the projecting knob of bone is small. In such cases, the wrist when viewed from the side will seem hardly any thicker than the palm of the hand, and for a distance of four inches up from the hand the forearm will show hardly any variation of size, all the bulk being in the upper-half of the forearm near the elbow. Such men can get big forearms but they have to work hard to get them. There are other men whose wrists are thick, with the bone apparent at the thumb side, and the development of the muscles seems to start right from the wrist. From the base of thumb, the tendon will be so big and thick that it gives the wrist a sort of square appearance. On the inner side of the forearms, about two inches from the base of the hand, there will be a small canoe-shaped muscle, which is rarely seen on men with thin wrists. Such men have but little difficulty in getting big forearms. Joe Nordquest has a wrist of this type, and when he bends his arm half-way and tenses all the muscles, his forearm for the moment looks almost as wide as it is long.

Enthusiastic muscle-culturists have a great habit of comparing arms. Two young fellows will get in a discussion about arm development, and end by rolling up their sleeves to show what their arms look like. Since the forearm is the first part displayed, its size and shape, or the lack of it, is what makes the first impression. A poor forearm is a great incentive to exercise, for a man will get so ashamed of a puny wrist, and shapeless forearm that he will spend a lot of time at exercises that will improve the appearance of the lower arm. Knowing that thin wrists make the arm look weak, there are fellows who always wear wrist-straps. The straps naturally add to the thickness of the wrist, and you would think that would make the rest of the forearm look smaller. The exact opposite is the case, for the effect of the wrist-strap is to make the fleshy or muscular upper part of the forearm look shorter and more massive.

Strong wrists are such an advantage that it is impossible to spend *too* much time at improving their shape and power. These big-boned, thick-armed men, conscious of the fact that nature has been liberal in the matter of handing out strength to them, will rarely take the trouble to develop their forearms to the limit. I have never yet seen a big man whose forearms measured more than $14\frac{1}{2}$ inches (when the whole arm was held straight) even though some of them had wrists which measured 8 or $8\frac{1}{2}$ inches. And I verily believe that with an 8½-inch wrist a man *could* develop a 15½-inch forearm if he cared to. On the contrary I know plenty of small-boned men, who have so resented their lack of size that they have developed forearms nearly *twice* the size of their wrists.

I know that in some quarters it is held that slender wrists and ankles are signs of an aristocratic ancestry, and that thick ankles and knobby wrists are indications of common blood. The fact is that if you inherit big wrists and ankles it is proof that your recent ancestors have, at least, done *some* useful work; or have been of the fighting, athletic type.

I can understand why a woman should cultivate slenderness in the extremities, but I never have been able to see why a man should consider thin wrists a distinction. Rather they are a mark of effeminacy.

CHAPTER V

Strength through Natural Advantages

HAVING dealt with the subject of big bones versus small bones, this seems a good time to discuss other physical characteristics which are in themselves natural advantages to the strong man.

Broad shoulders, for example, are a distinct advantage, simply because they are but another indication of a large and strong bony framework, which would be a good foundation on which to build muscle. There is, or should be, a relation between the size of your chest and the breadth of your shoulders. If you have a very small chest it would be unnatural for you to have very broad shoulders, and vice versa. When speaking of a man who is very strong, it is customary to say "he is a broad-shouldered, big-chested fellow." If you have broad shoulders you have at least three distinct advantages: (1) the vigor which you derive from the extra-size lungs in your big chest; (2) the extra room for muscle on and about the shoulders themselves; (3) the greater muscular leverage which comes from the wide spread of the shoulders.

Therefore any man with broad shoulders is potentially strong; that is, he has the *possibilities* of strength, which he may realize *if* he develops all the muscles of the shoulders. In another book, "Muscle Building," I have given instructions for obtaining that development; and so here I will merely explain that the width of the shoulders is governed not only by the size of your frame, but by the size and development of the deltoid muscles on the points of your shoulders.

106

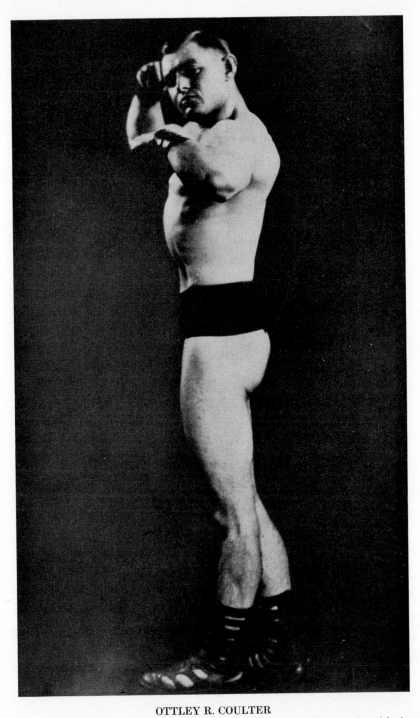

OTTLEY R. COULTER

The holder of lifting records for the light-weight class. His well-proportioned body proves that one need not be a giant in order to create lifting records.

In a true "Strong Man"—be he professional lifter or otherwise—these deltoid muscles are of extraordinary size. Whereas in the non-athletic type the deltoids are only a fraction of an inch in thickness, and so little developed that it is impossible to trace their outlines. In a "Strong Man" they may be anywhere from an inch to two inches thick. Just figure for yourself how properly developed deltoids will affect the appearance of your shoulders. The deltoid gets its rounded form because it covers the head of the upper-arm bone. If your deltoids are thin and weak, then the points of your shoulders will be bony, that is, you will be the kind of man of whom people say "Oh, he has shoulders like a hat rack"; but if you develop the deltoids so as to make them as strong as they can be, you will at the same time make them each an inch thicker, and that will add a clean two inches to your shoulder breadth. Without powerful deltoids no man can be really strong, for they are an important link in the chain of muscles which move the arm.

A man can have a big rib-box without very much deltoid development. He can have big upper arms, with but moderate deltoids; but if a man has highly developed deltoids, he is almost *sure* to have a broad back and big arms. For it is impossible to make your deltoids big and strong without making the arms and back bigger at the same time. The deltoids "connect up" the strength of the arm and the strength of the body.

Casual observers do not comprehend the importance of the deltoids. On seeing a lifter or a weight thrower, or a great gymnast they will exclaim at the size of his arms and the width of his shoulders, not realizing that it is the big deltoids which make the arms look so thick and which make the shoulders so unusually wide.

Since the deltoids lift the arms from the side, there

must be other muscles which pull the arms downwards; and these muscles are located on the back and the breast. Now, if the deltoids are big the muscles on the upper back are bound to be as big in proportion. When you see an athlete who has deltoids so big that each one looks almost as big as a baby's head, get behind him and take a look at his back, you will then find that across his back from shoulder point to shoulder point there are hills of muscle with valleys between; and if you let your gaze stray downwards you will note that from arm-pit to arm-pit the back is very broad and that the size of the body tapers inwards at sharp angles to the waist.

That is something that you see, not occasionally but invariably, in the true "Strong Man."

Knowing all this will perhaps make you realize the importance of broad shoulders. Sometimes you will be sitting in a train and some big chap will saunter in and sit down two or three seats ahead of you. And you will think it lucky that he got a seat to himself for his shoulders are so broad that they take up three-quarters of the room allotted to two people. You wonder if he is a football star, a piano mover, or perhaps a heavy-weight fighter. Whatever he is, you instinctively credit him with being tremendously strong. If you will recall what I have just told you, perhaps you will be able to figure out the different things which help make these mighty shoulders so impressive. If the shoulders are wide, take a look at his sleeves, and you will note that they are so cut as to make room for upper arms which are as big as some men's thighs. If he leans forward take a glance at his back, and see if it is not true that just below the arm-pits there are two bulging masses of muscle. Without doubt you have more than once seen such a man, and all you grasped was that he was broad-shouldered. The *next* time check up, and you will see for yourself that he has all the characteristics I have just listed, and that if one is missing he will somehow fail to give you the impression of being very strong.

The average man's shoulders are only 16 to 19 inches broad, whereas with some "Strong Men," athletes and heavy laborers you can take a 24-inch rule, lay it across their upper backs, and a man standing in front would not be able to see either end of the rule.

While every one knows the strength-value of broad shoulders, there are but few who ever consider the importance of broad hips to the strong man. In fact it is just the other way around. When a novelist wishes to endow his hero with all the desirable physical gifts, to make him speedy and shapely as well as strong, he will write: "He was tall, broad-shouldered and deep-chested, but with the trim hips that added grace and elegance to his figure." Others describing such a man, will say that he was "thin flanked."

Such is the structure of the hips that they are heavily muscled at only one place, and that is the buttocks. A man may have highly developed gluteus muscles, which is to say that the buttocks may project considerably, and yet his hips be narrow.

The hip-bones themselves—the pelvis—form a basin which acts as a sort of floor to the abdominal cavity. The bones of the thighs fit in sockets at the outer side of the hip bones. Which means that if the pelvis is wide the thigh bones are spaced wide apart, and if the pelvis is narrow the thigh bones are closer together. All of which affects a man's strength because it has a very direct influence on the firmness with which he stands. If the hips are broad, the legs are wider spaced and their owner will naturally stand with feet further apart than will a narrow-hipped individual. Also the wider-spaced bones will give more room for muscle.

Just as it's easier to upset a small, high table than to upset a low, broad table, just so is it easier to upset a narrow-hipped man than a broad-hipped one.

In a man the thigh-bones are not perpendicular but incline slightly outward from knees to hips. In a woman the thigh-bones incline outwards at a much greater angle. A woman's hips are broader in proportion to her height than are a man's, which explains why the upper part of a woman's thigh is bulkier than a man's thigh. And it also explains why some women are so strong in certain ways. A woman's strength lies almost entirely in her hips and thighs. As compared to a man's her arms and shoulders are weak, but in feats which require hip and thigh strength she can sometimes equal the efforts of a man of equal weight. I have seen girl fancy-dancers who could easily back a man across the room in a pushing contest.

According to those tables of ideal proportions, the hips of a man should measure only two or three inches less than the normal chest measurement at the level of the arm-pits; the difference being greater in a tall man, and less in a short man. Judging by what I have seen, this rule has no universal application. Arthur Saxon's hips were big and square and he probably came near the required proportions.

George Hackenschmidt had even bigger hips than had Saxon, but the difference in the size of their chests was even greater. I have not the figures before me, but I would guess that Hackenschmidt, whose bones were unusually large, had 42-inch hips and a 52-inch chest, which is a 10-inch difference. Sandow, with whose physique no one but himself could find fault, showed a 5-inch difference; for his normal chest was about 44 inches around and his hips 39 inches.

Even in the case of Oscar Matthes, who is about the shortest "Strong Man" on record, the difference was 5 inches, i.e., chest 40 inches, hips 35 inches. You may recall that Matthes' thigh measured 21 inches and that it seemed hardly big enough to fit in with his other measurements. The explanation is that with hips measuring only 35 inches it is hard to build up a thigh larger than 21 inches around. There simply is not room for more muscle. Owing to the outward inclination of the thigh-bones there is more muscle in the inside than on the outside of the upper part of the thighs. If the hips are narrow and the thigh-bones close together, the space for muscle is automatically limited. When you see it stated that a man has thighs measuring more than 24 inches around you can be sure that his hips are more than average width.

The great majority of men who do harness-lifting, back-lifting and platform-lifting, or who carry great weights on the back, or on one shoulder, have great thighs and wide hips. Such men have uncommon power in their loins.

If you are interested in outdoor games and athletics, you probably know that a man with natural advantages will excel at a particular event. It is well known that a long-armed man, if he get the proper pitching motion, can deliver a much faster ball than can a short-armed pitcher. And a tall, rangy man with long legs finds it easy to step over the high-hurdles in fast time, while a short-legged man has almost to make a high jump over each hurdle.

It has long been supposed, or believed, that there is some magic strength in extra long arms.

WARREN L. TRAVIS

The famous American strong man, who was a record lifter when the author
was a boy and who still is active in the iron game.

I have read books in which the author would introduce a man character whose purpose was to furnish the strength element. The description would be like this: "So and So was a man short of stature but famed for his prodigious strength. His shoulders were as broad as a platform, his chest round as a barrel and his muscle-knotted arms were so long that when he stood erect his gnarled hands hung almost to his knees." I think that the author must have had a gorilla in mind when he thought up this "Strong Man" character; for I have never seen a man of that description. I know lots of "Strong Men" but the ones who are long-armed are also long-legged. Once in a while I have seen a man whose body and arms seemed out of all proportion to his legs and hips, and the impression I got was that something had happened to arrest the growth of the upper limbs.

Big hands, particularly if they are long-fingered, are a distinct advantage in the performance of some feats of strength. This applies particularly in the case of a dumb-bell-lifter. John Marx had enormous hands with fingers so long that they would lap around a 3-inch bar. So in his act he used moderately heavy dumb-bells, but equipped them with very thick handles. A small-handed man who could have easily picked up with one hand a thin-handled 200-pound dumb-bell, could not possibly pick up Marx's bell of that weight, because his fingers would not circle the handle. So Marx got what was perhaps an undeserved reputation for strength.

I know men with small hands who have a prodigious gripping-power. There are small-handed gymnasts who can "chin" themselves several times in succession with any finger of either hand; which proves that their hands are strong. Given a proper-sized grip a small-handed man, who is strong in all other respects, will lift just as much weight off the ground with one hand, as will his big-handed rival.

Exactly the same principle applies to long arms. In some forms of wrestling, short arms, however thick and strong they were, would be a distinct handicap, because, if your opponent was extremely bulky, your arms would not be long enough to lock around him. On the other hand, I can conceive of a condition where long arms would be a disadvantage, particularly if your opponent got a wrist-lock and used against you the extra leverage of your own long arms.

As I said before, I do not know any "Strong Men" who have disproportionately long arms. Even when of normal length the strong man's arms *look* shorter than those of most men because of the thickness of the forearm, and the overlapping of the deltoids.

Strong wrists are indispensable to strength. In most ordinary feats of strength the object to be moved or lifted, swung or broken, is gripped by the hands; and those hands *must* be strongly coupled to the arms, so that there will be no break in the delivery of the power. A famous veteran, advising a new-comer in the professional ranks, said, "Young man, you will never be any stronger than your hands and wrists," and then proceeded to describe a few exercises to strengthen the wrists. And those exercises did not make the wrist any bigger but increased the strength of the hand-muscles, and particularly added to the size and power of the big bunches of muscle that lie in the *upper* half of the forearm near the elbow. Wrist strength is something that can be cultivated.

CHAPTER VI

"Quality of Muscle the Basis of Strength"

KNOWING that I am really interested in the subject of strength, many of those whom I meet—even chance acquaintances—will bring the conversation around to physical matters. One young man, a finely-developed chap, asked me to explain why he was not as strong as other men whose muscles were no bigger than his. Of course the answer was complicated, for there are so many different elements in strength. A man may have strong muscles but utterly lack any knowledge of applying his strength, so that he makes a poor showing against experts. He may have a one-sided, or unsymmetrical, development that makes him good at some tests, and poor at others. But generally the explanation lies in the *quality* of the muscles.

A muscle can be of high or low quality, just as may a steel spring. You can buy a steel spring which will have a certain degree of springiness, but which will ordinarily lose that quality under the strain of use. And you can but another spring of exactly the same weight and thickness which will have twice as much resiliency, and which will last indefinitely. The difference lies in the *quality* of the material and the superior process of manufacture.

You can take a piece of iron and by treating it in a certain manner, and by forging and reforging it, can convert it into steel, and make it several times as strong as it was before, without adding a particle to its bulk.

There is a way of developing muscle, which gives added size but surprisingly little added strength. There is another way which adds to the muscle's strength and leaves the size to take care of itself. And there is a third, and it seems to me an ideal way, which not only brings a muscle to its maximum size and greatest beauty of outline but also gives it enormous contractible power.

The size of a muscle is of course dependent on the number and thickness of the individual fibres which compose it; and size can be produced more easily than can strength. Just as the mind can be developed by giving it progressively harder problems to solve, so can the muscles be built up by teaching them to contract against progressively greater resistance. Take any man or boy who has drifted into the habit of using his muscles as little as possible. Start him with mild exercise and then gradually give him more, or longer or harder exercise, and his muscles will steadily grow in size and strength until the natural maximum is reached.

The last few years have witnessed the growth of a great interest in muscular development *for its own sake*. There is a way of producing muscular tissue in large quantities, of making various individual muscles big and shapely, but without adding very much to the strength of the muscle. This method, which is called by several different names, is really a system of development from "extreme contractions."

It is fascinating, because of the ease with which muscle is created, and disappointing by reason of the little strength that it brings. Undoubtedly it has its origin in light dumb-bell exercise. It soon became apparent that if a man used in his exercise, a pair of 2-pound dumbbells, the resistance offered by such light weight was not sufficient to make the muscles really work.

So the work was made harder in the following way: At the end of any movement the muscle was vigorously tensed by an effort of the will. This made the muscle contract to its full extent and it soon appeared that the more intense the mental concentration on the act of tensing the muscle, the more rapidly the muscle would grow.

The importance of the voluntary tensing overshadowed the value of the weights used; and so the small dumb-bells were discarded as they added nothing to the effectiveness of the method. To explain. If you clinch your fist, bend your arm, and bring your hand close to your shoulder the muscles called into play are the flexors of the arm, of which the principal one is the biceps muscle. Now, after the arm is bent, try and harden the biceps so as to make it stick up in rounded lump. Repeat several times, and your biceps will turn and get slightly sore. Do this every day for a month, and by the end of that time you will notice a considerable difference in the size of the muscle, especially when it is under tension. From day to day you will be able to put more force into the final contraction; and as that is a form of work each day the biceps will grow slightly larger. If you keep it up long enough you will get so that you can make the biceps protrude in a very imposing lump indeed.

Exactly the same thing can be done with most of the voluntary muscles. All you have to do is to learn the position most advantageous to extreme contraction; and then tense the different muscles strongly by an effort of the will. When a muscle is tensed, or used, blood is drawn to it, which accounts for the increase in size.

There are men who have obtained *fairly* big muscles in that way, but they never look really well-developed except when the muscles are tensed. When at rest these muscles, while fairly bulky, have a placid appearance; and entirely lack the clear-cut and shapely outlines that come from doing real muscular work.

A muscle so built up, when flexed to its fullest extent,

GEORGE JOWETT

The famous Canadian strong man, whose 18-inch neck blends with his massive
proportions, which can be appreciated by the above photograph.

will show a pronounced ridge, or hump, at its center portion—that is, midway between the tendons, or attach-
ments. The biceps, for example, will stick up almost in
a point, instead of in a high curve. When relaxed the
muscles are large only in the center and taper sharply to
the points where they join the tendons; and the tendons
themselves are not affected or strengthened by this
method of development.

A man who has developed himself by real work, has
muscles of an entirely different shape, and of vastly
greater strength. I have seen men with 15-inch arms
developed through the extreme-contraction method, who
had far less biceps strength then other men with 14-inch,
developed through exercises like "chinning the bar,"
"curling" heavy dumb-bells, or other movements in
which real work was done.

In order to develop the greatest strength, a muscle
must work against resistance through the whole range of
contraction. When chinning a bar, the biceps muscles
are continually at work, from the start when you commence to bend the arms, until the finish when your arms
are doubled up. All through the movement the arm muscles are lifting the weight of the body; i.e., overcoming
resistance.

There are "strength athletes" whose whole interest is
in the creation of high-quality muscles, and who care
little about the appearance of their muscles. Their desire
is to perform feats which require the maximum of muscular strength, and they deliberately train to increase
the strength of the muscle, and allow the shape to take
care of itself. What they care for is not how the muscle
looks, but what it will *do*. One of the best-known ex-
ponents of this theory was the late Arthur Saxon. In
some styles Saxon could lift more than any other man in

athletic history. There is a lift known as a "one-arm-bent-press," which is the method used by experts when they wish to "put up" a very heavy weight. The art of the lift consists in using the body muscles to reinforce the arm. In fact most of the elevating of the weight is accomplished by bending the body. I took a physician friend to watch Saxon perform, and when the "bent-press" was made, and Saxon's body was bent almost double to the side as he forced up a 314-pound weight, my friend exclaimed "that man must have phenomenally strong fascia."

The "fascia" are the thin fibrous sheaths which enclose the muscles. In your arm there is a fascia almost like a tight sleeve, which lies right under the skin and holds all the muscles together.

In the region of the hips and waist there are important fascia and I suppose it was to them that my friend had reference. You see he was not so much interested in the contractile strength of Saxon's muscles, as in the firmness of the fascia which prevented a displacement of the muscles of the waist region.

Saxon himself spent a lot of time in strengthening his tendons. He knew that his public performances required a lot of energy, and his theory was that light exercises only tired him, without making him any stronger. So when he practiced, he would do the sort of stunts which threw heavy work on the full length of the muscles, *and on the tendons;* such as the lifting, supporting and throwing around of enormous weights. And he would do each stunt only a very few times, and alternate his stunts with brief periods of rest, so as to prevent himself from tiring, and to conserve his energy. As a consequence, Saxon was never what you would call a beautifully developed man, although he was well-shaped and had a very rugged appearance. His muscles were sinewy rather than of the beefy type.

Particularly noticeable was the length of his muscles. The biceps of his arm, for instance, was big from its lower point in the bend of the elbow all the way up to where it disappeared under the deltoid at the arm-pit. The character of his work seemed to prevent any accumulation of fat, and his muscles were always plainly evident. No man ever made less effort to display his muscles, and yet few men have had stronger muscles. His upper arm measured about 17 inches when flexed, and his thigh about 24 inches; neither of which is extraordinary for a man who had a frame like his. His bones were about the average in size, but his tendons were much thicker than is usual; and I believe that the kind of work he did thickened and strengthened the tendons. Certainly I think that if he had cared for muscular development, he could have made his arms one inch, and his thighs two inches larger. With his bones and tendons he could have "bulked up" his muscles and, I feel quite sure, could have made them even stronger than they were.

The Boston athlete, John Y. Smith, was a smaller man than Saxon, but was of the same rugged, sinewy type, and had muscles of the same shape and character. So far as I can find out, Smith's training method was the same as Saxon's; and in his youth Smith was America's leading amateur "Strong Man."

While I am an earnest advocate of muscle-culture, I am willing to admit that there are very strong individuals who possess great strength, but who show no pronounced muscular development. Assemble one hundred men accustomed to heavy labor and you are sure to find, in that hundred, at least three or four who are far beyond the others in respect to bodily strength. They may be big, or just average in height; but always they are thick-set and well-knit. Their muscles are big, but not of the well-defined kind that we associate with "Strong Men." And yet when it comes to moving a 1,000-pound log, loading a huge crate on a wagon, or carrying a piano up stairs, these men are "there with the goods." Their strength must be due to their educated tendons which have been gradually developed through years of the kind of work which calls for great and continual bodily exertion.

The other day a friend told me of seeing a workman carry up one flight of stairs a bathtub weighing 1,500 pounds. Several men had to assist in getting the tub placed on his back, but once it was there he was able to walk away with it. When I asked what the man looked like I was told that he was not very big, but extremely well-made, standing about 5 feet 8 inches in height and weighing about 180 pounds. I would like to be able to study that man's muscles so as to determine where his strength comes from. Anyone would be foolish who attempted to prove that only those are strong who go to gymnasiums, or who practice physical-culture. I know, for a fact, that many of the new-comers to the ranks of professional "Strong Men" are recruited from among those who have developed their unusual strength by doing labor. And even a few months of intensive muscle-culture will not necessarily make one as strong as another bigger man who has spent years developing his muscles in the course of his daily work.

For my part, I am interested in the building of better bodies, I am more or less of an enthusiast on the question of muscular-development; and strength fascinates me. So quite naturally, I prefer a training method which promises results in all three directions—that at one and the same time improves a man's general build and his muscular development and increases his strength. In the line of exercise I prefer the kind that increases the muscular tissue, and strengthens the tendons. I like the kind of strength that can be converted into athletic ability, and I favor the variety of muscle that by its very shape proves that it has done work, and is capable of work.

Happily we can find many cases where the maximum of strength is accompanied by superlative beauty of figure; as in Sandow, Rollon, Arco, Redam and other famous "muscle-men."

My interest in the kind of muscle produced by different varieties of exercises, explains why I encourage, and sometimes incite my pupils to competitions to determine which of them can do the most "pull-ups" on a horizontal-bar; the most "dips," stretch the most rubber strands, or lift a 50-pound dumb-bell overhead the greatest number of times. When the competitors submit their records along with pictures showing their development, it is interesting to observe the effect of a vigorous exercise in developing and shaping the set of muscles chiefly employed.

You can build up any muscle, or group of muscles, if at regular intervals you give it exercise that is vigorous but not violent. "Vigorous" is somewhat indefinite, because an exercise which would be vigorous at the start, when you were undeveloped, might prove to be mild after you had gained in strength and development; and an exercise which would be dangerously violent for untrained muscles, would later on, after those muscles had gotten big and strong, be perfectly safe and easy of accomplishment. So any well-thought-out training system involves the introduction of the "progressive" element, the increasing resistance offered, or the increased

WILLIAM GERARDI
A Herculean athlete whose strength was exceptional. His 31-inch thighs
are the best developed that the author has ever seen.

vigor of the movement, without which no great gains in strength or development can be made.

The act of jumping affords us a very good example of the effects of violent versus vigorous exercise. For jumping can be used as an exercise, made violent or merely vigorous, and the resulting development bears a direct relation to the kind of jumping you have practiced. Jumping for extreme height is an exercise of the most violent character. When a man six feet tall clears a bar higher than his head, he performs a feat of strength, which requires a powerful and spasmodic contraction of the leg and back muscles.

And yet you will see in some illustrated sporting paper the picture of a group of star high-jumpers, and most of them will be tall and slender. Their legs are not heavily muscled, which makes you wonder where their strength comes from; and makes you doubt whether there is any basis for the theory that a muscle must be large in order to be very strong. The truth is, extreme high-jumping is one of those exercises which make the muscles strong without increasing them in size. The average college high-jumper really does but little practice. He jumps only during a few months in a year; practices perhaps only six weeks in all; and never makes more than two dozen jumps or "tries" in any one day. If he were to jump vigorously every day in the year, his thigh muscles would develop rapidly. I know this from my observation of professional jumpers, who invariably have magnificent legs. A professional rarely makes any terrific jumps; never practices with the idea of seeing how far he can project his body in the air; but displays his nimbleness through the means of "trick jumping." He will place a dozen barrels in a row and leap in and out of them in turn. Or he will place a dozen chairs in a circle around the edge of the stage, and, keeping his feet close together, will make a succession of standing-high-jumps, bounding over the backs of chairs like a bouncing rubber ball. All that requires much practice, which entails vigorous, but not violent, muscular contractions; and many of them. And because they practice many varieties of trick jumping they bring into action every muscle in the thighs, with the result that their legs become models of symmetry and size. I know one of these chaps who has positively the best-shaped thighs I have ever seen; so well-rounded that they look big from any angle. (You know there are men whose legs are thick from front to back and thin from side to side, and in other men the exact opposite is the case.)

All those trick-jumpers have wonderful thighs. And it does not seem to make a bit of difference whether their hips are wide or narrow, or if their bones are big or small. The man referred to above has a rather slender frame, which makes his thigh-development seem more wonderful by comparison. Also he is very strong, seemingly from possession of those legs, for he can lift heavy weights from the floor, and can carry heavy weights on his shoulder while he walks with a firm, even tread. The only other athletes who can equal the jumpers for thigh-development are some of the great fancy-dancers; and, after all, what is fancy dancing but continual jumping and springing? Ground-tumblers, who practice hours daily at handsprings, somersaults and like feats also get fine legs, because they use their leg muscles to propel their body weight.

I am one of those who hold that the strength a man can exert is largely controlled by the strength of the thighs; which is why I am devoting so much space to them. Ask an experienced friend how to develop your thighs, and he will probably tell you that all that is necessary is to practice squatting (the so-called "deep-knee-bend"), in which you first bend the legs and sit on the heels, and then rise up by straightening the legs. You try it and it seems very vigorous at first, for after a couple of dozen squats your thigh muscles cry out for a rest or even refuse to work. But you persist and after a week's practice you can squat 50 times without much trouble, and your thighs seem to have grown bigger and improved in shape. At the end of *two* weeks you can make a hundred repetitions; and at the end of a couple of months, your limit is gauged only by your endurance. This is the common experience, as there are men who can squat 1000, 1500 or even 2000 times without stopping. The disappointing thing is that at first your legs grew bigger and stronger rapidly, but when they reached a certain size the growth stopped; and they are not yet big enough to suit you. You may not have realized it, but the growth stopped just when the exercise ceased being one of strength, and became one of endurance.

According to our theory, the way to promote further growth is to make the resistance heavier and the repetitions less. This could be done either by resting a weight across your shoulders, or by squatting on one leg at a time. A still better way is to adopt the scheme of a young friend of mine. He had but a limited time in which to exercise and so had to concentrate. He made his squatting more vigorous by the simple expedient of jumping directly upward. As he stood up he would spring lightly upward; and as he landed lightly on the balls of his feet, would allow his knees to bend so that he would sink into the full squat, and from that position would again spring upward. So, instead of the thigh muscles just raising the weight of the body to a standing position, they had to contract strongly enough to shoot his body up in the air. He claimed that 30 such jumps gave one as much work as ten times as many ordinary squats, and produced much bigger muscles. Certainly he has developed splendid thighs in that way.

A couple of generations ago the first great American "Strong Man" adopted exactly the same principle to increase the size and development of his arms and upper body. This was the celebrated Doctor Winship, who was the Sandow of your grandfather's time. Winship lived at a time when there was no such thing as "home exercise," and so did all his training in one of those old-fashioned gymnasiums equipped with ladders, bars, rings, etc.

A favorite exercise of his was to mount the under side of an inclined ladder by successive "chins." Instead of going up hand-over-hand he would grasp a rung with both hands, give a strong pull, let go of the rung, flash his hands up and catch the next bar above. This is much harder than pulling your weight up slowly, as you have to "jump" your weight up by a strong contraction of the arm mucles. Consequently it produces bigger and stronger muscles, just as jumping in the air as you arise from a squat, gives bigger thigh muscles than mere squatting.

To mount a ladder as Winship did teaches one the knack of strong muscular contractions, because, as you come near the top of the ladder, if you miss you will take a 15 or 20-foot fall. Winship's muscles grew rapidly in strength; so to give them harder work he would skip a rung at each jump. This produced strength so rapidly that ordinary chinning became child's play to him and to chin the bar with one arm was no trouble at all. Then he went to going up the inclined ladder using *only one arm;*

and eventually reached the point where he could give such a terrific pull that he could mount three rungs at a time. Think of the prodigious power he must have had. It takes a "Strong Man" to "chin" even once with one hand but this Winship could actually pull so strongly with one arm that his whole body would be projected vertically upward. Probably he used similar schemes to develop the rest of his body. That his strength was not confined to his arms, is shown by the fact that in his exhibitions he would lift from the floor with hands alone, a platform bearing a dozen 100-pound nail kegs. And to do that he must have had immense strength in the back and legs.

To achieve the maximum of strength and beauty, it is necessary to practice exercises which teach your muscles to contract strongly, so as to develop the muscle throughout its full length from tendon to tendon; which can be done either through the use of strong springs or strands, weights, or just the resistance furnished by your own body weight. In addition it is wise to practice a little at "extreme contraction" exercises.

It is a great mistake to make your exercise *too* severe, or to make too much of it. If you wish to get the biggest and strongest muscles possible you will do better to make a few vigorous efforts than one violent one. Lifting a 300-pound weight from the ground six or eight times will develop the back more rapidly than lifting 500 pounds once. Stretching a 5-strand "exerciser" a dozen times will make the arm muscles bigger than doing the same thing only once or twice with a 7-strand; and much quicker than taking a 2-strander and stretching out 50 times.

CHAPTER VII

"Strength through Symmetry"

THE longer you study the question of physical strength the more you become impressed with the great necessity of symmetry—or all-round development.

The word "symmetry" implies a balance of parts. Most people think all that is necessary to symmetry is that the left half of the body be exactly equal in size to the right half. But there is more than that to physical symmetry; for as applied to the body symmetry it involves proportion. No man with big arms and shoulders and slender legs can be called symmetrical. And neither can a man who has massive legs, surmounted by narrow shoulders and puny arms. A man who is absolutely symmetrical will have shoulders of a certain width in proportion to his height; his legs and arms will have a certain length in proportion to his body; and moreover the girth of his arms will bear a definite relation to the girth of the chest, and the girth of the thighs to that of the hips.

Absolute symmetry has probably never been attained by any human being, and is only approached by some few noted "Strong Men."

There are men who go around the vaudeville circuits exhibiting their strength, who come close to being perfectly symmetrical. In fact they bill themselves as "perfect men" and they actually get more applause when they pose and exhibit their flawless forms, than they get when doing their feats of strength. The public, which after all, is composed of average human beings, loves bodily beauty and likes to feast its eyes on physical perfection; whether it is a "Strong Man" doing "classical

131

poses" in the lighted cabinet, a beautiful woman behind the footlights, or either one of the two on the beach in a bathing suit.

To resume the discussion. Has it ever occurred to you that his symmetry may account for a large part of a "Strong Man's" power? I can assure you that it is a fact. Further than that, I know that if a shapeless, undeveloped man takes up "exercise," and practices with the aim to make himself as symmetrical as possible, that as he attains symmetry he will also attain strength. When he becomes *unusually* symmetrical he will become *unusually* strong. This is because of the interdependence of the different parts of the body. You can perform an act which requires but little exertion by using the muscles of only one part of the body, but when you do something which necessitates putting forth a lot of strength, then the work is performed by, and shared by, a group of muscles. Thus you can take a tiny hammer in your hand and drive a thumb-tack just by moving the hand at the wrist-joint. If you had to drive a railroad spike through the three-inch top of a wooden bench, you would use a heavy hammer, grasp it firmly, raise your right arm high above the head and bring it down with great force. As you swing the heavy hammer upwards, the muscles of the forearm, the biceps, and the shoulder muscles would be at work, and as you smashed the hammer down, you would be using the muscles of the back as well as of the arm. Watch a man driving a drill with a long, two-handed hammer. As he whirls it up he will bend backwards at the waist, and as the hammer comes down he will bend forward from the waist; and just as the hammer hits the drill he will bend his knees slightly. By delivering the blow in this way he will get all the advantage of his weight *plus* the momentum of his swinging body and

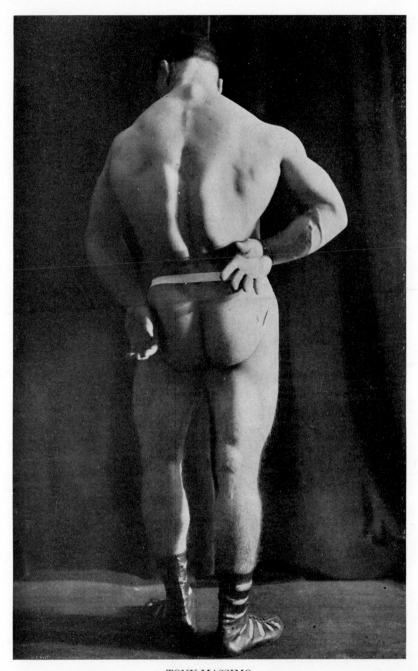

TONY MASSIMO

A famous professional strong man, whose Herculean physique is interestingly shown in the above photograph. Notice the exceptional trapezius development. He is a most remarkably developed athlete.

arms. In other words he reinforces his arm muscles with the muscles of his body.

A "Strong Man" when performing a feat which requires a great expenditure of strength, will instinctively bring into action just as many muscles as possible. Since all of his muscles are strong he can exert extraordinary power by making his muscles act in concert. That helps to establish the connection between symmetry and strength; or perhaps it would be better if I said, between all-round development and strength.

In another book of mine I recommended exercises which employ groups of muscles, instead of one muscle at a time. When exercised in groups the muscles acquire the power of working in concert; which is known as co-ordination. That, however, is but one of the beneficial results. A greater benefit comes from the increased strength and control of the joints. For almost every muscular contraction results in the movement of a joint. When an Irishman says, "More power to your elbow" he is actually wishing you more strength in all the muscles of your arm. When you say that man has a strong shoulder, you mean that he has strong muscles in the *neighborhood* of the shoulder.

In the case of any joint, power is located on either side of the joint. The biceps is only one of the muscles which bend the arm. There are muscles in the forearm which help. Just as the lower tendon of the biceps is attached to the bone of the forearm, several muscles of the forearm are fastened at their *lower* ends to the bones of the hand and at their *upper* ends to the bone of the upper arm. So when you bend your arm part of the power is supplied by the biceps pulling against the bone of the forearm, and another part by the forearm muscles pulling against the bone of the upper arm. When you "chin the bar" you can easily see both sets of muscles at work. As you bend the arms to lift the body, your biceps muscles will rise up in a hump on the front of your arm above the elbow; and at the same time your forearms will bulge out just below the elbows. For "chinning" develops *all* the flexors of the arm; and furthermore teaches your arm muscles to contract strongly in any kind of stunt or work in which it is necessary to bend the arm forcibly. That sort of strength is entirely lacking when the arm muscles have been built up by the "extreme contraction" method. I saw that clearly demonstrated when I put a couple of young fellows at curling a 50-pound weight. Each had arms which measured about 14 inches around the biceps. "A" had gotten his arm development by "chinning," rope-climbing and such *work*, and he "curled" the weight a couple of times without much effort. (In "curling" a dumb-bell, you allow the arm to hang by the side, and then without moving the elbow you raise the hand holding the dumb-bell, from hip to shoulder by bending your arm.) "B" was not able to curl the bell once; in fact he could not even *start* to bend the arm. "A"'s superiority was not due to practice, for it was, he admitted, the first time he had ever had a 50-pound bell in his hand. But his arm, *all* of it, from wrist to shoulder was used to vigorous work. Whereas "B"'s muscles had seldom worked against resistance. When working on his biceps, he would, as already described, bend his arm and force his biceps into a lump by an effort of the will, and meanwhile his forearm muscles were not even tense. And when he tensed his forearm muscles to develop *them*, his biceps were not even in action.

So much for the difference in strength. The difference in appearance was even more marked. "A" had a capable-looking, well-knit arm, which looked as though it could do something. But "B"s arm, notwithstanding the size of its biceps, was not impressive. It seemed to lack size right above the elbow, and right below the shoulder. His forearms did not merge properly into the upper arm.

Indeed, to an expert, it was very plain that his arm-muscles had been developed individually, and that they had very little power of working together with their neighbors.

That is just one illustration. I could give others, such as the peculiarly shaped and weak-looking thighs on men who have practiced but one kind of leg exercise; who have all the muscle in bunches right above the knees, and whose legs and hips seem to be hardly related to each other instead of being closely connected.

If you made a close study of the muscular make-up of a great "Strong Man" you would find a peculiarly well-knit condition in all his joints. Where the arm joins the shoulder you would find that his deltoid muscle would form a big cap over the joint itself, and that you could trace the lines of the deltoid almost to where its tendon fastens near the middle of the upper-arm bone. The big pectoral muscles would not show just near the breast-bone, but would extend right across the breast to the arm-pit. When he lifted his arm the breast-muscle would seem to flow into, or *merge* with the shoulder-muscle. His upper back, when in action, would appear to be possessed of more individual muscles than you would think possible, and as he moved his arms about, these back muscles would shift about in ever-changing con-tours, seeming to slip under, or play over each other.

And as for his legs, well: it would be difficult for you to say just where the thighs stopped and the hips began. Instead of the thigh muscles appearing to stop at the

top of the leg itself (as they do in ordinary human specimens), the muscles on the outside of the thigh would rise
in one sweeping curve, from the knee all the way to the
top of the hip-bone. And there they would disappear
under the great muscle at the side of the waist. On his
back there would be a great chain of muscles all the way
from the base of the skull to the back of the ankles. At
the top the *trapezius* muscles, of such shape and size that
they made the neck merge into the shoulders; then the
two great ridges of muscles along either side of the spine;
next the firm buttocks; then the great outward swell of
the biceps in the back of the thighs; and last of all the
powerful muscles of the calf. When you thus see that
every part of his body is adequately covered with muscle,
and as you watch him move any part of his body with
seemingly irresistible power, you comprehend how being
symmetrical and well-knit will add to a man's strength;
and it makes you realize that, with muscles, as with
everything else, "In union there is strength."

While we are on the subject, let me see if I can make
clear the way the muscles help each other out. You have
just, in imagination, been studying the back of a "Strong
Man." Let us suppose you admit its development and
that you ask him to display its strength. Thereupon he
places two chairs about four feet from each other; lies
down with his head and the back of his neck on one chair,
and his heels on the other; and allows you and two of
your friends to stand, one on his thighs, the second on
his stomach and the third on his chest.

This feat is possible only because he is so well developed along the full length of his back and legs. If there
were one weak link in the chain of muscles his body
would give under the weight. (Understand, in the first
place, that this stunt is a feat of muscular strength and is

not like some other supporting feats, where the burden
is carried on vertical bones. For when a man lies with his
head on one chair and his feet on another, all his bones
are horizontal).

In order to support the weight, the body must be kept
in one rigid straight line; and that is done in this case by
an almost violent contraction of the muscles of the back
itself and the muscles which run along the back of the
legs. Naturally the only place at which the body could
give way is at the hip-joints. You may argue that the
legs have little to do because even the greatest imposed
weight would not make the knees bend backwards. But
the legs have a lot to do, because in order to keep his
body from sagging the athlete has to dig his heels violently against the seat of the chair, and the force with which
he can press with his heels is governed entirely by the
strength of the buttocks and the muscles on the back of
the legs. Of course almost all the muscles of the back are
busy, for the spine must be maintained in a straight line;
but what I emphasize is that the muscles below the hip-
joint, that is of the legs, have just as much to do with
keeping the body straight, and the hips from sagging, as
do the back muscles which are above the hip-joint.

Now a man who can do that stunt must necessarily
have well-knit hips, and no joint can be well-knit unless
it has strong muscles on either side of it, and strong tendons crossing it. Now I can safely say that the average
physical-culturist cannot do that stunt because he has
not the necessary muscle. No amount of club-swinging,
or free-hand calisthenics will develop heroic strength in
the lower back, or in the rear part of the legs. But almost any big professional wrestler will do it, and so will
many tumblers, oarsmen, football players, and men who
do heavy labor.

EUGEN SANDOW

A most interesting pose of this most famous strong man when at the height of his career. Who can deny that the perfect balance and contour of his remarkable physique were the secret of his great strength ?

I long ago found out that it was the constant use of the back, which gave such great strength to some of those laborers; and my criticism of most "exercise systems" is that they pay insufficient attention to creating back-strength. A young fellow who exercises in his own room will spend half an hour doing exercises that afford vigorous work to his arms, shoulders, chest and upper-back muscles; and when it comes to his loins and the back of his legs, he thinks he has given them enough work if he leans over, swings his pair of 5-pound dumb-bells between his legs, and then as he straightens up, swings the bell overhead and leans backward. A work-man will think nothing of picking up, and piling a stack of cases weighing 50 or 75 pounds apiece. Or he will lift packages weighing as much and with a heave of his body, and a swing of his arms, *toss* them to another man standing on a platform above him. And the exertion is nothing to him because his back has become tremendously strong from doing that sort of work day after day and year after year.

Occasionally at a bathing-beach, one man will stand with legs firmly planted, a second man will sit on his shoulders, a third man climb up and sit on the second man's shoulders, and then some powerfully made young fellow will lean over, slip the back of his neck between the first man's crotch, and slowly stand up, lifting all three men with him. Naturally a strong neck is necessary, but there must be strong back muscles, and *very* strong muscles along the back of the legs. The strongly muscled legs form the anchorage against which the back muscles exert themselves. Now once more, a man who can thus lift three men on the back of his neck is the very fellow who can do the stunt of lying on the two chairs. And if you test him you will find that he can do another feat which employs the same leg muscles. Let him stand erect and take a firm hold of some firmly placed object, to give him a brace. Then ask him to raise his right foot backwards (without moving his knee) so that the right calf will extend out horizontal and at right angles to the thigh. If you stand on his right calf with one of your feet on the back of his ankle, and your other foot on the fleshy part of his calf you will find that your weight is not sufficient to force his leg downwards. Why? Because he has tremendous strength in the back of his leg, the biceps of the thigh, which has been developed through his constant handling of heavy objects.

All the foregoing was written just to give you an idea of what is meant by being "well-knit." If I had the space I could go on and give you similar illustrations showing that the same principle applies to all other joints; how for example, when a man has great strength in his sides—can keep his body straight against a great pressure that would bend the body sideways at the waist —you will always find that in addition to having great muscles on the sides themselves, he will also have great muscles on the outside of his thighs. That when a man has great muscles on the front of his abdomen, he will have great muscles on the front of his thighs, and so on. If you keep in touch with the sporting papers, you will notice many pictures of those Herculean heavy-weight wrestlers; most of them big men, developed from head to heel, and obviously possessed of great strength. Wrestling develops most, but not all of the muscles. When a wrestler takes the trouble to supplement his exercise with stunts that develop the upper extremities and which still further cultivate his body and leg-muscles, *then* you get a sample of super-power and super-shape like George Hackenschmidt.

Chapter VIII

Strength from Perfect Digestion

THERE is no question I am asked more frequently than "Mr. Liederman, what shall I eat to make me strong?"

Perhaps you remember the fairy-tales you read in your childhood days. The hero of the tale ate some magic food, or drank some magic potion, and would immediately become so strong and brave that he would go out and clean up an army single-handed. I assure you, there are people today who almost believe that kind of thing. I once met an undersized young fellow who was quite convinced that if he could only hit on the right kind of food-preparation, in a couple of months' time he would become a sort of combination of Sandow and Jack Dempsey. And when I told him that I knew of no such food or drink I could tell he thought that I was "holding out on him." I have never yet met a "Strong Man" whose digestion was poor. Their powers of digestion and assimilation are on a par with the power of their muscles. Now, whether their muscular strength comes from the perfect working of their organs, or whether their perfect digestion comes from their muscular strength, it would be hard to say; but undoubtedly there is a connection. I have observed that the very strong amateurs and professionals with whom I am acquainted have two noticeable characteristics. They eat in a deliberate manner and masticate the food thoroughly; and they have a marked preference for concentrated nourishment. Also it must be admitted that some of them are what you would call "large eaters."

It stands to reason that a large man with powerful muscles, and who uses those muscles, will require more nourishment than will a small man who uses his muscles but little. It is further noticeable that when an active and powerful man changes his occupation to some inactive employment his appetite will gradually become less. A "Strong Man" does not deliberately eat a lot of highly nourishing food with the fixed intention of keeping up his strength. He does so *instinctively*, for the exercise or work at which he spends his strength gives him a grand appetite, and he instinctively satisfies that appetite. Under certain conditions you, the ordinary man, do exactly the same thing. You have been working all week, and on some crisp Saturday afternoon you go off on a hike, climb a big hill, play 18 holes of golf, or perhaps take part in a game of football. For two or three hours you are continually using your muscles; which means you are spending physical energy in large quantities. When, after a bath and rub-down you sit down to your Saturday evening meal, you discover that you have a "whale of an appetite," and you amaze and dismay your family by the amount of food you eat. If you ate a meal like that after a day in the office you would probably have unpleasant consequences in the way of a headache and indigestion. But after vigorous exercise the organs will take care of a lot of nourishment.

If you take vigorous exercise regularly you develop a regular appetite; and along with the appetite comes a definite increase in the ability of the digestive organs to turn food into energy and muscular tissue. And these "Strong Men" by virtue of their employment and physique require a lot of food to keep them going. And so does a stevedore, or a ditch-digger or any other man who uses *all* his muscles continuously. When a man eats unusual quantities his friends will say "he has an appetite like a farm-hand."

If you go to college and are on the football or rowing squad, you are made to eat at the training table; where you are provided with food that is easily digested and which provides nourishment. You are given no choice, as the dishes are selected by an experienced trainer. It seems to me these very "Strong Men" develop an instinctive taste for that kind of food. Go to lunch with one of them, and while you are hunting over the bill-of-fare for some dainty dish that will tempt your appetite, your companion will fix the waiter with a stern eye, and say, "Bring me a big steak, a lot of potatoes and a pitcher of milk" or perhaps, "Bring me a big order of pork and beans, and when I am through, bring me another." When it comes time for dessert he will wave away the French pastries and either have ice cream, pudding or some kind of fruit-pie.

I sometimes wonder if anyone besides myself ever noticed the similarity of the diets of an invalid and a "Strong Man." A man recovering from an illness will be given broths, beef tea, milk-and-eggs, ice-cream, milk-toast; and as he gets stronger, meat. That is just the kind of dishes the "Strong Man" naturally prefers. I know professionals who at the end of an exhausting act will consume large quantities of beef tea, or some meat extract. They claim that it immediately restores their strength; the explanation being that the juices of the meat are assimilated very rapidly.

An invalid can "keep down" ice cream, when his stomach will reject everything else. Some of these "Strong Men" positively inhale ice-cream. I asked one of my Herculean friends, who thinks nothing of finishing every meal with a "quart of vanilla," why he ate so much ice-cream. All he had to say was that it somehow "reached the spot."

EUGEN SANDOW

The above interesting pose is from an old photograph which I, fortunately, secured and the muscular formation portrayed is so interesting that I feel the reader is given a rare treat despite the condition of the picture.

Another professional of my acquaintance always breakfasts exclusively on milk-toast; his ration being about a loaf of bread toasted and put in a quart of hot milk. A tubercular case, a consumptive, when sent to a sanitorium, is made to consume an "egg-and-milk" at regular intervals during the day, and this simple diet seems to check the disease and restore the wasted tissues. A "Strong Man" who happens to like eggs will think nothing of eating half a dozen at a meal. As to the regularity of their meals—well, there is no such thing. They will eat at any time, before or after a performance, and sometimes both. They eat whenever they are hungry— and some of them are hungry all the time.

Now I suppose all that is very unscientific, and that it seems to contradict all the theories of those authorities who insist that the human body thrives best on a "balanced ration," that every day one must absorb a certain variety and quantity of different food elements; who insist that only one kind of bread is nutritious, or that one must eat exclusively of fruits and vegetables. All I am doing is to tell things as I have seen them; and I do not mean that there is nothing in what those food experts teach us.

A busy banker might be much healthier, if instead of eating rich and expensive dishes, he confined himself to a diet which was scientifically planned in quantity and food-values. But that is no reason for believing that a "Strong Man" should eat exactly the same quantity and kinds of food. No one would expect the average banker, or lawyer, to carry a thousand pounds of iron on one shoulder, or to match his strength against that of a team of horses; and neither should anyone expect a big husky to maintain his strength or create new power, on the diet of an indoor worker of average physique.

There are some people who simply cannot understand that the man who has power and muscles of phenomenal size and strength is almost bound to have digestive organs of equally exceptional power. I believe that the almost perfect digestion of those who are very strong is mostly due to the development of the muscles in the neighborhood of the digestive tract. Like other teachers of physical culture, pupils are sent to me by physicians, with the requirement that I prescribe an exercise program to cure chronic constipation, or chronic looseness of the bowels. I know that one kind of exercise will relieve constipation by promoting the activity of the liver and intestines; and that another kind of exercise will cure the other condition through toning up the organs and regulating their secretions; and that still other exercise will improve the quality of the blood.

In such cases I notice that an exercise which benefits the liver will develop the muscles at the sides of the waist; and that by the time those muscles have grown large and shapely the liver will be working properly. Also that the development of other muscles near the waist-line will "tone up" other organs.

As the real "Strong Man," the symmetrically developed, well-knit chap, is equipped with a wonderful set of muscles encasing his digestive organs, he is immune from any digestive troubles. He is even better off than that. With him it is not just a matter of being free from organs that work properly or inproperly, for he has organs that function with immense vigor. I hope you see what I mean. There is an immense difference between being merely free from disease, and being immensely vigorous. Undoubtedly there are business men of advanced age who have never taken any more exercise than they could help; who have "never been sick in their lives"; who have never become either emaciated or grossly fat. Why? Because they are blessed with almost perfect digestion and assimilative processes. So there *is* a connection between good digestion and continued health. And there is just as close a connection between an extraordinarily vigorous digestion and extraordinary bodily strength.

In concluding this chapter I wish to emphasize the fact that any exercise program which is designed to increase the size and strength of your muscles, *should* add to the permanent vigor of your digestive organs. Therefore, when you exercise you should keep a careful watch on your appetite. If you have a good appetite and crave nourishing foods, you are on the up-grade and can expect rapid increases, if you satisfy that appetite. If on the other hand, you lose your appetite, it means that you are over-exercised or under-exercised; and that your muscles will not grow, nor your strength increase until the appetite returns.

Chapter IX

The Importance of Big Lungs and a Strong Heart

NOWADAYS there is a great deal of talk about blood-pressure. One would almost think that it was the sole index of health and condition. I can remember when it was the correct thing to say, "Oh a man is no older, or younger than his arteries." Meaning that if an elderly man had elastic walls to his arteries he had a good chance of continued life and activity; and that if a middle-aged man had arteries with weak and brittle walls, he was practically an old man, much older than his years would indicate.

Now, I can give you a maxim, which is, "*No man is stronger than his heart.*" And this fact is so well known to professional athletes of all kinds, that they sedulously avoid the over-exertion that might cause heart-strain. If you are among an audience watching the performance of a "Strong Man" you are almost sure to hear some wiseacre remark, "That fellow won't last many years doing that sort of stuff; some day he will burst his heart." You see, it is just like it was about digestion. The average man simply cannot realize that the performer's heart is just as much stronger than the average heart, as his biceps is stronger than the average.

The heart is an involuntary muscle, and for that reason many believe that while it is possible to train and strengthen the voluntary muscles, it is utterly impossible to train and strengthen the heart. It is true the growth and condition of the heart cannot be directed as simply and easily as is the case with voluntary muscles.

Everyone knows that it is possible to train the lungs,

yet their action is controlled by partly voluntary muscles which go on acting automatically whether you are walking or sleeping.

Did you ever stop and think just what is meant by the expression "getting into training?" Do you realize that the primary object of an athlete's training is to strengthen his heart and lungs? After a season of loafing you report for football practice. The trainer looks you over, sees your condition and gives orders that every day for a couple of weeks you jog several times around the circumference of the playing-field. He knows that will take off the soft fat and harden your muscles; and, more important still, will improve and strengthen your heart and lungs. If you are "out of condition" you will not last long in a hard football game; no matter how much you know about it, or how strong you are. For who can exert his strength, or show speed if he is winded, or if his heart is pumping away above its normal speed? Try it for yourself. Run as fast as you can for a quarter-mile and then try to wrestle with a man weaker than yourself. Because he is fresh and you are winded, he will throw you all around. To resume, the first day you start at your jogging, you will be lucky to go the full distance without stopping. You may have to pause a couple of times for rest, and when you finally finish your heart is thumping against your side and you are puffing heavily. Each day the work gets easier, and at the end of the short space of two weeks you will be running with steady, even strides, and when you finish you are breathing heavily, but are not in the least distressed for breath; and your heart is functioning powerfully and rhythmically. What you have accomplished is to strengthen the heart and lungs by daily vigorous use. What gratifies your trainer is that instead of being "dead on your feet" at the end of the first

JOE NORDQUEST

Displaying his famous 18-inch upper arm. Joe's reach is 68 inches and this photograph interestingly shows that the larger the arms become, the shorter they look.

period, you can now run swiftly, charge vigorously, and tackle fiercely all the way through the game.

This sounds as though I were talking of endurance instead of strength. Well, what is endurance except *continued strength?* With a weak heart it is possible to continue mild work for a long time without ill effects, but impossible to do "strength" stunts for even a short time.

Take a man with a weak heart, and you can walk him 15 miles in 5 hours on a level road, and it will neither exhaust him nor affect his heart action. But walk him up the side of a steep mountain, and before he has gone a mile, his heart will be beating so violently that it would be dangerous for him to continue. Up-hill walking is "strength stuff" because you are lifting your weight as well as propelling it. Make a weak-hearted man sprint a quarter-mile at top speed and you may kill him. The exertion of great strength for short periods calls for a stronger heart, than mild exertion over long periods. To run 100 yards in ten seconds is harder on the heart than running a mile in six minutes. Now we will get back to the "Strong Man." When one of these Samsons walks around while supporting half a ton on his shoulders; when he pushes up a huge and heavy dumb-bell; or when he pulls around a pair of horses, he is getting exercise in its most concentrated form.

Any exertion reacts on the heart, and the heavier the exertion the stronger the heart must be, if it is to react properly. And yet a trained "Strong Man" will carry his half-ton of weight, put it down and wipe the sweat off his brow; and while his chest may heave with the strong lung action, his heart will be going only a few beats per moment faster. Consider what he has been doing. While supporting the weight all his biggest mus-

cles were strongly tensed. The muscles in his back and
sides stood out in big lumps and bands, and his thigh
muscles literally bulged under the severe strain. When
a muscle is highly tensed, the blood-vessels which serve
it are squeezed together, and it takes a very strong heart
to keep the blood flowing through these compressed arteries and veins. The fact that the performer can do
such a feat, without any evidence of distress is the best
possible proof that his heart is *very* strong.

Sometimes in a gymnasium some casual visitor will
attempt to equal some feat which has just been performed. Perhaps a trained athlete has pulled so strongly
on the handle of a lifting machine that the indicator
registers 800 pounds. The visitor thinks that must be
easy, because the athlete did not even breathe hard; so *he*
will try it, and tug as he will, the indicator will not go
above the 400-pound mark. Hating to be shown up in
that way, he again grasps the handle of the machine,
sets his feet firmly, takes a long breath, and pulls with
all his might and main. As he struggles, he first gets red
in the face, then his eyes pop out, and the veins in his
neck and forehead protrude. Luckily at that point any
of the experienced men present, will force him to quit;
asking him if he wants to break a blood-vessel. That
chap may go away fully convinced that great exertion
is bound to wreck one's heart; or he may come back and
practice on the machine, always keeping well within his
growing strength. If he does *that*, he will find that his
lifting muscles (legs, back and shoulders) will grow
steadily bigger and that in some odd way his heart has
become immune to the usual effects of heavy exertion.

I, who have watched hundreds of "Strong Men" perform and practice, have never seen any one of them force
himself so hard that he got red in the face; or had to hold

up the performance while he rested his heart and lungs. What would *you* think if a famous "Strong Man" puffed heavily, or got purple in the face as he "did his stuff." You would think that was a poor kind of strength.

As it happens these "Strong Men" fascinate you because they can do such incredible things without distress. Even a feat which makes their muscles bulge like masses of metal does not seem to affect their regular breathing.

And it is by his breathing that you can usually gauge the condition of a man's heart. The heart and lungs have a related action. Do anything that requires vigorous exertion, and as your lungs work more rapidly your heart will do likewise. Examine the chart of a fever patient and you will see that any marked increase in the rapidity of the pulse is accompanied with a proportionate increase in the rapidity of the respiration. I claim that if I watch a man moving about—exercising and working— I can always tell whether his heart is weak. If his heart is weak, he will puff even at such mild exertion as climbing two flights of stairs. If you make him talk just as he reaches the top, he cannot speak without gasping. For with a weak heart one cannot control the lung action, while with a strong heart one *can* regulate the breathing. An acquaintance of mine has an odd habit which demonstrates my point. He is a bear on keeping himself in condition. Every morning he will wait on the street, near one of the elevated-railroad stations until he hears his train come to a full stop. Then he will tear up the stairs, rush through the gate and board the train. He has to hustle or else lose his train—and he has never lost it so far. If I happened to be on that train he would sit down beside me, and commence to talk in a perfectly even voice, without the slightest sign of the exertion he has just performed. The explanation is that he has a very strong and solid heart. If you pressed him he would admit that his heart was beating rapidly, but there was no trace of labored breathing. If the heart is strong the lungs will work steadily, even if the exertion is so great as to make the heart beat strongly and rapidly. But if the heart is weak, even a short period of real exertion will put the lungs out of control. And as most "Strong Men" breathe quietly after finishing their terrific feats, I *know* their hearts are strong.

There are all kinds of weak hearts. A heart may be damaged; its walls strained; or its valves "out of gear" so to speak; and a heart of that character can be made stronger by judicious exercise, but its possessor is debarred from getting *very* strong, and is debarred from exercises or games where great strength is required. No man with a heart like that should try and row a 4-mile race or take part in a long bout of wrestling. Many weak hearts are weak because their owners are weak. Often a fat man with flaccid muscles will have a heart which is muscularly weak; so if he overtaxes his weak and untrained muscles he will overtax his weak and untrained heart. But since there is no *organic* trouble, such a man can by progressive exercise, strengthen his heart; just as much as he strengthens his back, leg or arm muscles; and there is nothing to prevent him from becoming *very* strong and highly athletic.

There are still others who have neither any organic or muscular weakness of the heart, but are afflicted with what is know as a "nervous heart," in which the heart will jump or flutter at any sudden alarm, and will also fail to react properly after exertion. As an example of that condition I can repeat for you a story told me by a professional athlete. This man, with his two partners, performed an acrobatic and tumbling act. The biggest

man of the other two was a powerful and enduring man;
in fact, he *had* to be so as he was the "understander"—
the bottom man—who supported, caught, and generally
threw around, his two lighter partners. So strong was
he that he could do the heavier part of the act half-a-
dozen times a day if need be, and still be fresh at bed-
time. But unfortunately he was a heavy drinker—a
periodic—never drank while on the job, but if there were
two or three weeks between engagements, would slip off
by himself, get drunk and stay drunk. A few days before
the next engagement was due, my friend would hunt up
the deserter and *work* him to put him back in shape.
When the "understander" returned he would be in piti-
able condition. All the usual outward signs; and in addition his hands and limbs would tremble if he tried to
use them, and he would jump almost out of his skin if a
door banged, or an autoist blew his horn. Of course, the
other two saw to it that he got no more liquor; and when
they started in to practice they could work him only on
easy stuff and for a few seconds at a time. In a day or
two his shakiness would disappear, his strength and endurance would come back to him and by the time the
show began he would be his old self again; and no one
would have suspected that his heart could ever trouble
him. But just the same at the end of one of his "bats,"
he had every symptom of the so-called "nervous heart."
It is interesting to know that of late years some of the
great European specialists have cured cases of apparent
heart-weakness by gradually accustoming the sufferers
to the strenuous sports of mountain-climbing and weight-
lifting. Evidently the treatment is for the purpose of
strengthening the muscular fibres of the heart, since it
would hardly be safe in case of dilation or leakage.

As to the lungs, the same public that suspects the

JOSEPH NORDQUEST

Displaying the most unusual control of the back muscles. His enormous arms can
also be appreciated in this unique posture.

heart-condition of the "Strong Man," willingly concedes
the size and power of his lungs. Indeed the evidence of
lung-power is so plainly visible as to be undeniable. One
of a "Strong Man's" most striking attributes is his ability to *expand* his lungs. It is true that some performers
have over-emphasized their true, or lung, expansion by
adding to it the muscular expansion of the upper back
muscles as described in my book "Muscle Building."

But without resorting to such dodges, the really
"Strong Man" can show three or four times as much
lung-expansion as can the average man; and twice as
much as most athletes can show. Make the average "non-
athletic" stand erect, with his arms hanging by his sides;
have him expand his chest just by filling his lungs with
air, and he is lucky if he can expand his chest as much
as one inch. Athletes put under the same test will show
two or three inches' expansion, while many of these
"Strong Men" can show a genuine lung-expansion of
four or six inches; and sometimes even more than that.
(The above method is the only sure method of showing
the genuine expansion. Most people when asked to expand the lungs will hunch the shoulders and spread them
apart. This does not give one a bit more lung-room, but
it does spread and contract the upper body muscles and
give a false expansion.) If a spirometer is used to
measure the lung capacity, it will prove that while the
average man will inhale only about 200 cubic inches of
air, the "Strong Man" will inhale 350 to 400 inches. You
must remember that the "Strong Man" with his broad
shoulders and big rib-box, has more lung-room to start
with. To those assets you have to add his unusual power
of expansion, and you get the secret of the forced capacity of his lungs. The extra lung-capacity is a valuable
asset in more ways than one. The "Strong Man" with

his big rib-box breathes more deeply than others do. While they sit at rest and are breathing quietly they may take in only 80 to 100 cubic inches of fresh air at each respiration; whereas the big fellow takes in twice as much revivifying air at each breath. In other words his *normal* breathing-capacity is twice the average; just as he can take in twice as much air when under forced draft, so to speak. It is almost impossible to make a small-lunged man understand the muscular energy that comes from the possession of big lungs. You have doubtless noted the great difference which your surroundings make in your energy. In a stuffy, unventilated room you feel "loggy," and the slightest movement is an exertion. When you are in the fresh air you feel buoyant and en-ergetic. A big-lunged man has at all times—only in greater degree—the energy that you feel when out in the open. There is still another advantage which the big-lunged man possesses which comes from the size of the rib-box itself. It is just such a mechanical advantage as comes from the possession of broad shoulders, wide hips, or big bones. On a good-sized rib-box the muscles attached thereto will be longer than is usual and will have more room to develop and thicken. Hackenschmidt's "globe-like" chest was accounted for, both by the size of his exterior muscles, and by the high-arched and capa-cious rib-box which underlay those muscles.

Happily anyone, be he large-boned or small-boned, can get a big, roomy chest if he practices deep-breathing. Most people think that the only reason for cultivating the lungs is to promote endurance; whereas big powerful lungs actually add to a man's strength because they add vastly to his energy.

I have known track-athletes, football players, base-ball players and oarsmen to die of lung trouble and of heart trouble. But I have never heard of but one real "Strong Man" who succumbed to either of those maladies; and that was Louis Cyr, who died from angina pectoris, induced by his excessive corpulence.

CHAPTER X

The Secret of Nervous Energy

WHEN you hear it said of a man, that "he possesses a great amount of nervous energy," you can be assured that he has the power of expanding every ounce of strength that is in him, and then some.

We all know that muscles, at least the *voluntary* ones, do not contract of their own volition. All muscular contractions follow nerve-impulses which originate from the motor-centers of the brain. The legs of a dead frog will move, if you apply a galvanic current to the leg muscles. The twitching is caused by the stimulation or irritation of the electric current.

Our muscles have always the *power* to contract; but are motionless until the nerve message, or stimulus, is telegraphed from the brain.

There are individuals who possess nervous force, or what might be called "muscular will-power," in a very marked degree; and these individuals may be either of a stolid and phlegmatic, or of a highly nervous, temperament. Usually the latter is the case. There are slender men and women, who possess greater strength and endurance than their size and development would lead you to believe. Various physiologists have given as an illustration the case of several different men competing at "chinning the bar." A well-muscled man without much nervous energy will chin several times in succession and at the fifteenth repetition he will have exhausted his strength, and his muscles are so tired that he cannot again raise his body. Another, and much frailer, man will show the same signs of muscular exhaustion at the end of the eighth repetition. By an effort of the will he will force himself up the ninth and tenth times, and then when you feel sure that he must be "through," he will manage to slowly and shakily drag himself up a couple of times more. I also have seen that happen, and I noticed a couple of things that other writers have failed to mention. In the first place I saw the first man, the one with the purely muscular strength, was in good condition at the end of the test; and that after a few minutes' rest he could have made a second trial and done almost as well as the first trial. And I also observed that when the slender, "nervous-energy" man finished his test, his whole body was shaking, and his arm-muscles quivering so violently that he could hardly hold on to anything. Which made me doubt whether it was wise to thus force the muscles beyond the normal limit of their strength. This nervous energy is a fine thing *to have in reserve*, so that it can be used in great emergencies; but I am convinced that if a man thus forced his strength, and spent his energy thus prodigally in his daily exercise, or his daily work, he would soon become both muscularly and nervously exhausted.

A thoroughbred horse has nervous energy in a high degree and he will, when forced, keep on running long after an ordinary horse would be exhausted. But the result of such forcing is that the horse becomes "utterly spent." Remember that word "spent," and be careful when exercising never to *spend* your energy beyond your power to replace it.

Sometimes you will find a man who has great muscular strength and to that adds unusual nervous energy. When you get a combination like that in one man, he is almost sure to be a star. Of such ability was a young friend of mine. A lad of extraordinary development and great lifting power, he was extraordinarily good at mak-

TONY MASSIMO

A most remarkable photograph showing the muscles acting in coordination, besides expressing their beautiful contour, and their massive proportions.

ing what lifters call the "two-arm-press"—that is, where
you grasp a heavy weight in both hands, and push it
slowly to arm's length above the head. He was so good
that at any time he could beat all ordinary competition,
but he never extended himself unless it was absolutely
necessary. Once in a while he would cut loose. It might
be against a particularly strong competitor, or just with
the desire to see whether he could improve his record.
On such occasions he would go the limit at his favorite
stunt. After pushing up the bar-bell oftener than you
would think it possible, he would call on his hidden re-
serves of strength, and force many more repetitions by
sheer nervous energy. And it never seemed to hurt him.
To be sure he was anything but high-strung; being short
in stature, and very chunky in appearance.

A great expenditure of nervous energy is often accompanied with a marked loss in body weight. Thus a man
in hard muscular condition will take part in an important
football game, and because he plays with such intense
fierceness, and literally gives his team "all he has," he
will finish the game five, ten, or in extreme cases, twelve
pounds lighter than when he started to play two hours
previously. And almost invariably he has to be given a
week's rest to recuperate his energy.

I have seen young fellows dressing for the game, and
their muscles were clean-cut, and there was no visible fat.
And at the end of the game, when they would stagger
back to the dressing room, they would be positively
haggard in the face, and their bodies would be gaunt;
the muscles having lost their roundness, and having a
corded appearance. If they had been measured I doubt
whether the tape would have shown their muscles to be
any smaller. What they had lost was the very slight

amount of fat which is present in the body of every healthy and vigorous person.

The kind of man who is small and slight and yet has enormous strength is met most frequently in the pages of novels. In actual life you rarely meet him.

Often when reading, I have met a character of whom it was said, "in his slender frame he concealed the strength of a giant," but although I know hundreds of amateur and professional athletes I have never met but two men who answered that description. The first of them is a well-known physical-culturist, short of stature and without anything about him to indicate that he is very strong. And yet he can apparently exert strength in unlimited quantities, rarely failing to accomplish any stunt he undertakes. He can lift as much weight as can men who are twice as big, and is a wonder when it comes to finger-pulling, or "chinning the bar" with one finger at a time. Although his muscles are not very big they are long and extremely clean-cut, for like most people who have great nervous energy, he never accumulates any fat no matter how much he eats and drinks.

The other man is six feet tall, not noticeably broad, and weighs but 160 pounds. In street-clothes he looks more like a student, but when he strips you then understand where his strength comes from; for his body is covered with muscles like interlaced wire ropes. You can trace the outline of practically every muscle throughout its whole length. His flesh is extremely hard, and the muscles look lean and stringy. His claim is that his muscles are of extra length, and that while they may lack girth, they contain as many cubic inches of fibre as do the shorter and thicker muscles of a shorter and heavier man. He is admittedly a very strong man indeed; not one of the very top-flight; not in the class with men like Hackenschmidt and Nordquest, Saxon or John Y. Smith—but *very* much stronger than 999 men out of 1000 of his own weight.

But just the same he sort of worries me. Every time I see him work I get the impression that he is forcing himself too hard; that his strength is more nervous than muscular. Of all the very "Strong Men" I know, he is the only one who seems likely to have a breakdown in middle life. My impression is that he trains too hard, and too constantly. He is like a man who is not only spending his own income, but borrowing in addition. Some day he will make a draft on his strength and be without the physical resources to meet it. To my mind those two men are just the exceptions that prove the rule that "real strength" comes from fine proportions, solid organs, and a great muscular development. Since 99 out of every 100 "Strong Men" are well-made and magnificently developed, we can assume that the way to become strong is to exercise in a way that creates ideal shape, and great muscles.

That the condition of the nerves has much to do with strength cannot be doubted. The average "Strong Man," be he lifter, wrestler, lumber man or sailor, is usually of an even disposition, not easily rattled or excited, and very calm and self-controlled. And yet every thing a "Strong Man" can do, can be matched by the nervously deranged. One of the most startling instances of this was the case of a young woman who went insane in early maturity. She was a small, slender creature of the fragile type, with no more strength than is possessed by other women of her size. After her mind went wrong, and they had to confine her, she had attacks of maniacal frenzy. And in those attacks she would perform incredible feats of strength, bending the iron bars in the win-

dows, tossing around husky attendants as though they
were infants; and on one occasion ripping a heavy iron
grating out of the wall. This case is I believe famous,
and there are other cases almost as remarkable.

What I cannot understand is how the muscles and
organs of an insane person can possible stand the strain
put on them. Consider the young woman just mentioned.
If when in her right mind, she had attempted to bend a
stout iron bar by means of a sudden wrench, her body
would not have stood the strain. In the first place her
fingers would have straightened out; because when normal she had not enough grip to hang by one hand from
a ring. In the second place, she would have in all probability have pulled a tendon, or even torn the fibres of a
muscle. Thirdly, the exertion would have been sufficient
to have caused a rupture of the body-wall; and lastly,
she would have undoubtedly broken a blood-vessel. But
when in a frenzy, her muscles and tendons were apparently endowed with the strength of steel, and her heart
and blood-vessels in some way become immune to injury.

Naturally none of us value our strength more than
our sanity; but instances like this are almost enough to
shake the faith of the most confirmed muscle-culturist.
But there they are, and you cannot ignore them.

Before passing on, let me refer to these "human magnets" who give public demonstrations of their strength,
or more often of their resistance to the strength of others.
They deceive many, but I can assure you that all they do
is based on known principles of scientific leverage; together with the assistance of confederates. They are no
more capable of doing real strength stunts than a sleight-
of-hand-performer is of actually controlling occult forces.

To get back to examples of nervous force. It is not
hard to add instances. There are sane men who under

great stimulus, can exert twice their normal strength. I know a couple of amateur wrestlers who in friendly competition can show but little strength and who soon tire. But if something happens to get them "fighting mad," they are immediately transformed. They tear into their opponents like tigers, and amaze you with their sudden access of strength and endurance. You sometimes hear of a man, who in a desperate fight suddenly "goes berserk," and for a few minutes becomes a raving terror. The expression dates back a thousand years to when the old Vikings before a battle would, by means of liquor and mental excitement, work themselves into a sort of frenzy. Since after such a display, or attack, the fighting man has almost no recollection of the wonderful things he has done, it is fair to assume that he has not "been himself"; that in fact he has been temporarily frenzied; gone mildly insane, you might almost say.

Contrasted to that you have the case where the individual lacks control of his nerves to such an extent that when under the paralyzing influence of fear or embarrassment, he loses his strength to such an extent that he seems almost helpless. Once there was a young amateur baseball player, who played third-base and was famous for the strength of his throwing-arm. He could "burn then across" with such speed that the first-baseman sometimes had to beg him to ease up. Well, this chap attracted the attention of a big-league scout, and was signed. He got his first chance on the day of an important game, where there were thousands of spectators. The regular third-baseman got hurt, and this chap was rushed out. On the next ball pitched the batter hit an easy grounder down the third-base-line. Our man gathered it in very clumsily, drew back his arm, and though he apparently put a lot of force in his throw, the ball

JOSEPH NORDQUEST

The world's record holder of 301 pounds for the left-arm bent press overhead.
The seat of his remarkable strength can be readily seen in the above pose.

floated as far as the pitcher's box and fell to the ground. Of course he was yanked out; for even the spectators could see that he was having an uncontrollable attack of stage fright. He could give no explanation of his own loss of power, except that his arms and legs felt as though they were made of lead; and that the slightest movement required a great exertion. And yet he was a powerful, well-set-up young fellow.

There was another chap who impressed me by his physical strength. He always practiced by himself, being a shy sort of fellow; but after I got to know him well enough I visited his little gym. To tell the truth I was a little disappointed because he failed to lift nearly as much as he had claimed he could. But I could see that he had great possibilities; and I went back a second time, and third time, and on the last occasion he did some strength-feats as remarkable as I have ever seen an amateur perform. Soon after that, I witnessed the performance of a team of professional lifters; and I felt sure that this young amateur could beat them at their own pet stunts. So I invited them to pay me a visit, and I arranged that my young friend should drop in casually. I chuckled to myself, as I thought how he would surprise those noted professionals. *I* was the one who got the surprise. For my young friend failed to make even a respectable showing, and in some lifts could not lift half as much as he would ordinarily. Of course my other visitors soon got wise to the little game I had tried to put up, and they kidded the poor fellow so that he went entirely to pieces. Afterwards I said to him, "You're a fine guy to let me down like that." He colored up and replied, "Mr. Liederman, I couldn't help it. I was scared stiff, and it seemed to me as though I had left all my strength at home."

That was another case of pure nerves, for the lad really was exceedingly strong, and had as fine a set of muscles as one would want to see. And I know that his heart and lungs were O. K. Again those are exceptions to the rule. Exceptions so startling that they are worthy of remark.

A man who is famous for the strength of his body invariably will have great control over his muscles, and almost invariably an equal control of *himself*. If they have nerve attacks, they are the kind which *increase* the muscular power instead of diminishing it.

Perhaps their public appearances have made self-control a matter of second-nature to them. This applies equally to a circus-performer, a champion wrestler or a great college football player. All of them have learned that in order to do their best they have to ignore the crowd and concentrate their mental and muscular power on the matter in hand. So they learn to control themselves; and, as I have already said, the "Strong Men" of my acquaintance are just as remarkable for their self-control—their mental poise—as for their bodily strength. Perhaps it is the knowledge that they *are* strong, the consciousness of their power, that gives them their control and courage. There *is* something about great strength that adds to one's vitality and nerve. For I have often seen a timid feeble man improve his nerve, and gain in courage and self-assurance as his muscles grew bigger and his strength increased.

Chapter XI

Building Vital Force and Reserve Energy

I HAVE found that the cultivation of muscle is an easier matter than the creation of strength. To increase the size of a muscle, or a small group of muscles, requires only time and concentration; whereas the upbuilding of strength requires those two things *plus* the judgment which comes from experience. That explains why a man who puts himself under the guidance of a capable instructor will increase in strength far more rapidly than will the man who attempts to teach himself. In other books, I have described the exercises which develop the different muscles; so in this chapter I will write about the increase of bodily strength which comes from a properly regulated training-program.

An aspirant for physical strength and muscular development may train for months before he finds out whether he is on the right track. Instead of keeping in the main highroad and making steady progress towards his goal, he may unwittingly run off on a switch —get side-tracked—and arrive nowhere.

A young fellow bursting with the ambition to be strong will undertake some too strenuous program; plow right in and work hard from the very start. He has been told that this program has enabled others to become enormously strong, so he thinks it should do the same for him. In a few weeks everything goes along swimmingly. His arms get bigger, his legs sounder, and muscles seem to mysteriously spring out at unexpected places on his body. He finds that every day he is getting stronger and stronger; and he goes around telling everyone how fine he feels. He becomes an ardent advocate of physical exercise, and urges his friends to follow his example. But after a few weeks, say at the end of the third month, he commences to feel a little less "peppy"; and if he continues his hard exercise, he is finally forced to admit that he not only has stopped gaining but seems to be slipping. His daily exercise which was his greatest pleasure, now becomes sheer drudgery and he dreads the approach of the hour when he has to exert himself. If he is wise, he will realize that he has been rushing things too much and is overtrained; but that sort of wisdom comes only from experience, and this is his *first* experience. Notwithstanding the fact that he can feel his energy decreasing, he persists at his program. "Why should I give it up," he asks himself. "Look what it has done already!" Even if he has come to a halt, no one can deny that he is bigger and stronger than he was three months ago. And to quit for a while would interfere with his sacred program; for he has figured it out that if he did so much in three months, at the end of six months he will be just so much bigger and so much stronger. And, though he would not admit it for the world, he has it all doped out that at the end of the year he will make Sandow and Hackenschmidt and those other fellows take a back seat. So he keeps on, and his muscles not only fail to grow bigger, but actually get a little smaller. True, they are *harder*, but are not getting stronger as rapidly as he had hoped. Worst of all he keeps getting more and more tired, and his friends instead of complimenting him on his fine appearance, have taken to inquiring whether he is sure he is well. If he persists (and lots of those fellows do), then before long he reaches the point where he has to stop whether he wants to or not. It becomes a case of either quitting his job or quitting his exercise, for he has not strength enough for both. So with a long sigh he foregoes his ambition; puts away his exerciser; and decides that this exercise business is all a snare and a delusion; and that he was unwise to try and improve on nature. For a few days all he does is to tend to his job, but he soon finds that he is sleeping with a complete and gratifying soundness and wakes up feeling alert. His appetite comes back, and his meals look so good to him that he does them full justice. He puts on weight at the rate of a pound or so each day; his cheeks get some color in them; his step becomes springy and the feeling of strength singes through him. Thereupon his kind family proceed to say, "Just see how much better you look and feel when you don't do those foolish exercises!" However, the young man does not concur in this opinion, for with half an eye he can see that he is now a better man physically than ever before; *ever* so much stronger than before he exercised. So impressive do his muscles look that he gets out the old tape-measure and is gratified, but not surprised, to find that his arms and legs are actually bigger than his previous best, and by golly! unless he eats less and gets some kind of exercise he will get actually *fat*. The temptation gets too strong for him and he retires to his room, gets out his exercising-machine and decides that just one stunt won't hurt him any. Now he *is* amazed, for he finds that he can lift more, pull harder, push more forcibly than ever; and that stunts which used to be very difficult are now as easy as pie for him. (Nine chances out of ten he will get back on his program as quickly as possible; and unless he has learned his lesson, is quite apt to repeat his unpleasant experience. In the tenth case he will not exercise any more, and as the days go by he loses the feeling of great exhilaration and strength, and gradually drifts back to his old untrained condition.)

EUGEN SANDOW

Photographs of Sandow are always interesting, for his perfect proportions
have acted as an inspiration to millions of physical culturists.

The foregoing is not a story which I have made up out of my head, but is something that I have known to happen not only once, but in dozens of cases. It even will occur to a wise professional athlete under certain conditions.

A long-distance specialist will enter one of these six-day affairs. For six weeks previous to the event he will train carefully and scientifically, doing track-work, or road-work, to harden his muscles, and to put his heart and lungs in condition for the great test. But not once in that time will he *over-do*; for he is training so as to go to the starting post with immense energy in reserve. And he does! But as the contest proceeds you can see him literally fade. His small store of fat will be burnt out of him; his face gets haggard, his muscles stringy, and his bearing that of an old man. Toward the end of the sixth day the underfeeding, lack of sleep and over-exertion have taken their toll, and he becomes a sample of utter physical exhaustion. He forces himself to finish—win or lose—rather than forfeit his share of the gate money.

When the race is over he is put to bed, and sleeps and sleeps. If he wakes up, he is given nourishing food, and then he slumbers off again. When he has gotten his fill of sleep, he devotes the next few days to heavy feeding. His appetite is something to stagger you. If he weighed 160 pounds at the start of training, 150 pounds at the starting post, and 125 at the finish, it is likely that three weeks *after* the race he will weigh 175 or 180 pounds.

I offer that as a parallel case to that of many men who start to exercise. If you ask me what "six-day racing" has to do with strength, I will admit that it seems to be more like an endurance test; but endurance, as we have already seen, is nothing but continued strength. If you further object that a six-day-racer is rarely a very strong or powerful man, I have to reply that he at least has a tremendous stock of energy; and remind you that I am now writing about the building up of reserve energy.

Let us switch to another viewpoint. It is possible for a man to make most remarkable gains in size and strength of any one set of muscles and to keep on gaining without a single setback. It is conceivable that one could increase the girth of one's upper arm from eleven to sixteen inches, vastly increase its strength, and do this without any loss of general energy, or any ill effects whatever. For if you confine your work to one part of the body, most of the beneficial effects are shown just in that part, and some in the neighboring parts; and the *bodily* exertion is not great.

It has been proven that vigorous movements, repeated only a few times, tend to increase both the size and strength of a muscle much more rapidly than will a violent movement repeated once; or a mild movement repeated one hundred times. Now, since there are comparatively few muscles in the upper arm it takes only a few different exercises to bring those muscles into action; and since each exercise has to be repeated a few times, it becomes possible to develop the arms to their fullest extent by exercising them only five or ten minutes every twenty-four hours. As the muscles grow bigger and stronger, the exercises will naturally become easier of performance; and then all you have to do is to increase the resistance against which the arm muscles are working; without making it necessary to make more repetitions, or to spend more time. Under such a plan, and if you do little other exercise—you can build up your arms until they are so big that when you don a bathing-suit your arms will simply dazzle the eyes of your friends. But don't forget that all you will be is a man with strong arms, not a strong *man*. Even the biggest arms will not enable you to *jump* any higher, if your legs are still small and weak. Nor will they enable you to lift, or carry, a lot of weight if your lower back is still weak.

I have seen some extraordinary cases of special development built up on this one-at-a-time plan. It happens that the pectoral muscles on the front of my chest are rather well developed; and apparently they attract attention, for others comment on their size and shape. They seemed to particularly impress a young pupil of mine. He asked me, "Mr. Liederman, won't you tell me how to get a pair of chest-muscles like yours?" I assured him that that was part of my job; and instructed him how to do a couple of exercises using very stout rubber cables, and along with these to practice "dipping" on the floor, and on the parallel bars—and to take but mild work with the rest of his body.

He worked with enthusiasm and determination, and although it is only a few months since he started, he came in the other day and displayed to me the most remarkable pair of breast muscles I have ever seen. Remember that when he started his breast muscles were barely visible, whereas now when he flexes them they mount up in two huge bosses of muscle and look almost as though you had cut a football in two lengthwise, and placed a half on his chest each side of the breast-bone.

"Dipping"—particularly the parallel-bar variety— is strenuous work, and employs the muscles of the upper back, the upper arms and the shoulders. But it calls particularly on the breast muscles. So I was not surprised to see that this lad's shoulders were broader than before and his arms much bigger. So thick had his breast muscles become, that they added considerably to the diameter of his chest. They made his chest very deep from front to back. His chest girth is 42 inches normal, something wonderful for a young fellow of his height.

The "dipping," being vigorous arm-work, had built up his upper arms so that they measured a clean 15 inches. But it was apparent that the increase in arm-girth was a sort of by-product. When I freely admitted to him that his chest muscles were bigger than mine, he came back with, "How much does your arm measure?" I told him, "Oh, about 16½ inches"; and then as I anticipated, he said, "Now tell me some exercises to give me an arm like yours."

I have accordingly given him some special arm-exercises, and I fully expect that before long he will come back with a pair of 17-inch biceps—especially if he follows my directions. I knew that it would be unwise to add too much work to his daily program, and told him to cut down on the "dipping," and that he could do this without worrying about losing his chest-development. For while it takes a lot of hard work to develop a muscle to its limit, you can *keep it* at its limit by only a little work. Actually this lad had been doing 150 "dips" per day—75 on the floor, and 75 on the parallels. I told him to cut down to fifty, twenty-five each way. That would give the breast-muscles sufficient work and would leave him a lot of energy for his special arm-exercises. To you or to the man of ordinary development, "dipping" twenty-five times seems like a day's work in itself, but you must remember that this chap has muscles so big and strong that 25 "dips" is no more exertion to him than climbing three flights of stairs is to you. This unusual young man has great ambition, and is gifted with a large stock of patience. If he sticks to his present plans of developing one part of his body at a time, it make take a couple of years before he has brought *all* his muscles to the same standard of perfection that his pectoral muscles now possess; but at the end of that time he will truly be a "muscular-marvel," and should be terrifically strong.

However, there are but few who are willing to spend two years at becoming thoroughly developed. A beginner does not want to postpone his entrance into the "Strong Man" clan as long as would be necessary under the above plans. The desire is to become a strong *man*, which entails all-round strength, and not special or local strength.

Personally I believe the best plan for the beginner is to start with exercises of a rather mild character, for then one can include movements which develop every part of the body, and supplement those with other general exercises which use almost all the muscles simultaneously. This sort of work yields but comparatively small results so far as muscular growth is concerned; but its great advantage is that it limbers up the joints, gives elasticity and some strength to the muscles; enlarges the lungs, strengthens the heart; and best of all improves the general condition of the whole body, and inures it to fatigue. Because none of the exercises are severe, even a long period of exercise will not cause the fatigue which comes from over-exertion. This kind of exercise is just what is prescribed for a man who "just wants to keep himself in condition." But at that it is the best start-off even for the boy, or man, who intends to train for great strength.

After the body has been thus prepared, more vigorous exercises are in order. So long as the progressive principle can be adhered to, the kind of apparatus is not limited to one kind. Adjustable bar-bells are certainly convenient. Heavy pulley-weights can be made to do. Gymnastic apparatus can be used, and a schedule of

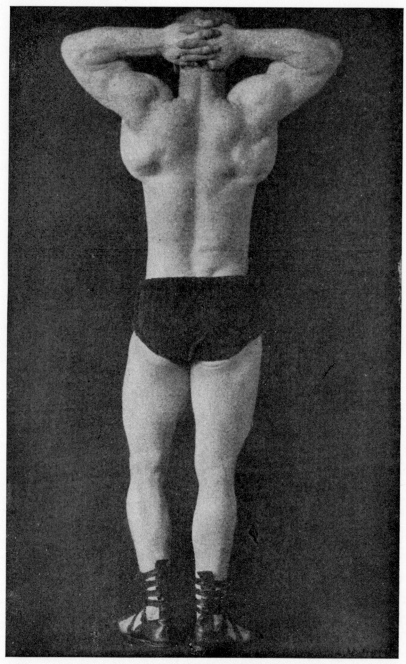

ADOLPH NORDQUEST
Displaying the remarkable development of the upper back.

progressively difficult exercises be figured out to suit.
And when there is positively no apparatus of any kind
to be had, it is still possible to use the weight of one's
own body to furnish the necessary resistance.

But as soon as you undertake real "strength exercises"
you must be on your guard. Not against over-strain so
much as "over-work." No fixed schedule will suit in any
and all cases. There is always what they call a "personal
equation," which in this case is a complicated one. Even
when the aspirant for strength is organically sound, such
factors as one's age, shape, size of muscles, digestive
power, resistance to fatigue, and power of recuperation
must be considered.

The *internal* factors are the most important. A man
who has a perfect digestion to start with, will put on muscle more rapidly than another man whose digestion has
to be improved as he goes along; and a man who starts
with a strong heart and big lung-capacity will stand a
lot more work than the man who has to *develop* heart-
and-lung-power.

And then there are men of a calm, unexcitable disposition, who seem to quickly recover their strength and
have a power to quickly rebuild muscular tissue; and
other nervous people who take longer to "come back,"
after the fatigue of developing exercise.

Every man must watch himself carefully during his
first few weeks of muscle-building exercise. I do not
mean the mild preparatory exercise, but the vigorous
work which follows it.

A prizefighter preparing for an important contest
will spend six weeks in training for the battle. Experience has shown that an athletic man can be brought to
the very top notch of condition in that length of time.
And if the training is too prolonged, the athlete will

become over-trained or "stale" and will lose energy.

Although the fighter is being trained for a temporary condition, while the strength-seeker is training for *permanent* growth, the training principle is the same in both cases. Just as the fighter's trainer keeps a close watch on his charge, so as to discover any signs of waning energy, so must you carefully observe your own condition, and your reactions to exercise and training. We have seen that in order to promote muscular growth it is necessary to adopt a progressive schedule. Give a muscle progressively harder tasks to accomplish, and, *providing your condition is right*, nature will attend to making that muscle bigger and stronger. But if great and rapid progress is to be made, there must be a certain balance between exercise, rest, and nourishment taken; otherwise even the best system of exercise ever devised will not yield results.

Most beginners become fascinated with the progressive schedule of exercise and are apt to follow the schedule blindly, regardless of results.

When I first became interested in exercise a kindly old gentleman said to me, "Young fellow, all you have to do is to 'chin the bar' once the first day, twice the second day, three the third day, and so on; and before long you will be able to chin 100 times in succession and you will get a great pair of arms." Now the old man told me that in simple good faith, and I accepted it as a great idea. I went right to it, and actually succeeded in following the program until the fifteenth day; and after that everything went wrong. Instead of giving my biceps muscles a rest I did just the opposite. Convinced that the trouble was not with the schedule, but with me, I practiced "chinning" at intervals during the day, forcing myself to the limit at each session. As a result of this hard work I succeeded in the next month in getting my

record up to twenty "chins," but I was so utterly disappointed by my failure to keep advancing at the rate of
one a day, that I lost faith both in myself and the
progressive idea.

The whole trouble was that neither of us knew enough.
If the old party had told me to *gradually* increase the
severity of the exercise, and to be content to increase one
repetition each *week*, then it is quite possible that I could
have made 52 successive "chins" at the end of the year;
as nature would have been given time to build up the
necessary muscular tissue.

I regret to have to say that the average beginner, when
embarking on a progressive schedule, will show but little
more judgment that I did. When he starts out he is
effectually "sold" on two ideas. He understands that in
order to get all the size and strength and development
he craves, he must exercise *regularly*, and he must exercise *progressively*. So he makes a mighty vow, that come
what may, he *never* will skip an exercising period, and
he will keep always abreast of the advancing schedule.
He may even go so far as to plot out his schedule for
weeks in advance, making a chart, which calls for so
many repetitions of an exercise on this day and so many
more on the next. So many strands to be stretched this
week, and one or two more the week following. Or so
many more pounds to be lifted as the days go by; or
perhaps an ever-increasing number of "dips" and "chins"
and "squats." And each day he will "check off" each
exercise as he completes it and he has a blind faith that
if he can only keep up with the schedule, nothing in the
world can prevent him from rivaling Hercules.

Now, it must be admitted that for a time, while the
work is still easy, everything will go along swimmingly,
and the development and strength which makes itself

evident, seems to prove the value of progressive work, leads to high hopes, and encourages one to continue. It is only when the daily exercise becomes so severe that it tires you, that there is any danger of over-work. And as soon as your body is over-worked, progress and growth will cease for the time being. There is one infallible way of telling whether you are on the safe side and that is your enjoyment of the work. I do not mean the mental gratification that comes from keeping up with the sacred schedule, but the actual feeling of *physical satisfaction* which comes from a good muscular work-out.

If after your exercise, your bath and your rub-down, you feel fit to battle for a kingdom, then your schedule is right. If, on the contrary, your exercise so exhausts you that it is hours before you again feel brisk, then the work is too heavy, and you must either take a rest, or else reduce the severity and amount of the exercise. Progressive exercise is positively the only road to great strength, but after all is said, the important thing is not the way the schedule progresses but the way *you* progress. So you must learn how to make the schedule fit you, rather than to sacrifice yourself to the schedule.

On the other side of the question, it is plain that unless you do exercise with a fair degree of regularity, progress will be nil. You won't get anywhere if you exercise by fits and starts, for muscle and strength will not put in an appearance until your body recognizes the demand for those attributes. Go barefoot every day for a month, and before the month is ended, the soles of your feet will have toughened. Shovel coal for an hour every day and before long the palm of your hands will become horny and calloused. But if you go barefoot, or shovel coal only occasionally you get nothing except cuts and blisters. So it is with exercise. *Within certain limits* the supply will equal the demand; providing the demand is constant.

However, when building up strength, while regularity of exercise is important, strict regularity is a mistake. Suppose, for example, your program requires you to exercise once in 48 hours, and for an hour at a time. You can best spare that hour in the evening, probably just before you go to bed. Say that this week the exercise periods fall on Monday, Wednesday and Friday evenings. On Monday and Wednesday everything is lovely, for you have been sitting at your desk all day, and your body is crying out for exercise. But on Friday you are sent around the city to interview a lot of clients, and you have to walk miles and miles, and you have a date for dinner, followed up by dancing until far after midnight. When you go home at 2 A. M. your body is tired. You can get only a very few hours of sleep at most, and the idea of staying up another hour and forcing your weary muscles to do a lot of hard work is utterly foolish. But I give you my word that I have known it to be done by some of these over-zealous enthusiasts. Why in a case like that the proper thing is to say,"Oh, well, this is not Friday night but Saturday morning, and I will take my workout on Saturday night this week."

The   general rule is, that the more vigorous an exercise, the less often it has to be done. That is the great beauty of progressive strength-exercises. When you have made your arm so strong that you can reach up, grasp the limb of a tree and "chin" yourself a couple of times with one hand, then all you have to do is perform that stunt two or three times a week. You will keep growing in strength and the exertion is of such short duration, that a minute later your arm-muscle has gotten back its energy. And yet only a few weeks previously while build-

JOSEPH VITOLE
The world's record holder in the teeth lift. Though weighing only about 150
pounds he recently lifted, with his teeth alone, 550 pounds.

ing-up that arm strength, you had to use both hands to "chin" yourself, repeat a lot of times, and require a correspondingly long time to get back your strength and your energy.

Therefore you have to guard against working too frequently; and you have to also learn to regulate the amount and kind of exercise you take at any one time. A great deal depends on how much time you are willing to spend at practice. If you are a real dyed-in-the-wool enthusiast you can practice as the professionals do; which is to distribute the work over a couple of hours, of which only twenty or thirty minutes are spent at actual work, and the rest of the time taken up by the in-between rest-periods. If you prefer to spend most of your free time at your other hobbies, and can spare only two or three hours in the whole *week*, then you must be content with slower progress, and had better adopt the special program which I will recommend later on in this chapter.

The ideal way to exercise is to arrange things so that on the days you exercise, you do a series of movements that provide work for every part of the body, one part at a time. But in that case you must allow plenty of time for rest. There are hundreds of young fellows who prefer to spend three evenings a week at the gym, instead of going to the movies or dances. And if they can do it, why not you? True, they go to the gym for the fun they get out of it, whereas you would go for serious work. And since there is no room to do serious work on a gym floor that is monopolized by the basketball players and "class drills," you will do better to take your exercises at home.

It occurs to me that I may have given a wrong impression when I laid so much stress on the necessity of rest periods between exercises. It sounds as though those exercises were so terribly severe that after each exercise or "stunt" you would have to spend several minutes "coming to," as it were.

I harp on this subject, because it is vital that I make you understand the difference between training "just for condition," and training for *strength*.

A man training for condition will go to his gym, his club, or his athletic-field, and for an hour or so will move around so briskly that he will sweat profusely. And the more he sweats, apparently the happier he is. If he works so strenuously that finally he is standing in a pool of perspiration, he will consider that he has done his duty by himself, having his shower and rub-down; and then go around bragging about what a "grand work-out" he had. He said it! Literally he has *worked himself out*, and that is exactly the thing the strength-seeker cannot afford to do. If your idea of training is that you must dash from one exercise to the next with the sole purpose of "getting up a sweat," then I can tell you right here that you will never get *very* strong, or well-developed until you give up that idea. I have seen powerful young men preparing themselves for a "Strong Man's career," stay in their training quarters for an hour and in the course of that time do only a dozen exercises, and although those exercises were of an extremely strenuous character, these young men would never work themselves up to a profuse perspiration. They had sense and experience enough to realize that one cannot build up muscular tissue, if one sweats to a degree which makes one lean; nor build up energy if one is continually spending all the energy in stock. Of course, if the weather was extremely hot, they would perspire just as any healthy person does, but as their muscles were in superb condition they would perspire less than most do.

When training, a "Strong Man's" custom is to first "warm-up" the muscles by a little light work, because one can no more do feats of strength when the muscles are cold, than will the engine of your automobile develop real power if *it* is cold. After the light work the athlete will perform some vigorous stunts. It may be lifting a heavy bar-bell from floor to chest, and then pushing it aloft; and repeat. But the instant the work of lifting becomes too difficult, he stops and walks around for a couple of minutes. He is not particularly out of breath, because he selected a weight that was heavy enough to make him really exert himself and therefore couldn't be lifted many times in succession. And he is not particularly tired because he deliberately stopped before he had to. He could have lifted more, but he is saving his strength. After a couple of minutes' rest, he works another set of muscles, this time preferably some of the smaller muscles, like those of the forearms; since that requires considerable local exertion, but no great output of bodily energy. And then another bit of hard work, such as a dead-weight-lift that requires great and powerful contractions of the thigh and back muscles. Then more rest, and perhaps some little special work for the calves of the legs; as that also can be done without a great output of energy. And so on. And always he saves until the last his hardest stunts—the ones that require the use of almost all the muscles, and which therefore use up energy in large amounts. Never does he make the mistake of doing the hardest exercises, or stunts, in the first part of the training hour. If he did that, he would be working under the disadvantage of having diminished his strength and energy, and of working with tired muscles. If you happen to be a track-athlete, you know that if you had entered your name for the high-jump and the three-mile-run you would prefer to do the jumping first. You could do the necessary dozen or so jumps, and if you had a few minutes' rest you could still show your very best in the distance-race. But if you first ran at your best speed for three miles, and then after fifteen minutes' rest had to compete in the high-jump, you would most likely make a miserable showing. The long-continued exertion of the three miles would have sapped your energy and taken all the spring out of your legs.

(I realize that is a rather poor comparison, as the same man is unlikely to enter in two such different events as a high-jump and a distance event. But it will serve to make you understand why one training to develop strength and reserve energy always saves his hardest work for the end of the training hour.)

Now I have more than once watched several experienced young huskies training in company, and vieing with each other in the performance of difficult stunts and arduous lifts. Suddenly one of the strongest would walk towards the showers, and if the rest said, "What is the matter, Gene? Quitting so soon?" he would reply, "Yep. Had enough for today. Feel just right. Gotta save myself you know." Or perhaps it will be, "Up late last night, and got hardly any sleep. Haven't got the pep to keep up with you fellows today."

None of the rest will coax him to return as any one of them is apt to do the same thing any day. One and all of them have had enough experience to know it is foolish to force oneself to do hard stunts when not feeling right; especially if there is no real emergency or necessity.

A professional "Strong Man" carries the principle of his training right into his "act." Most "strong acts" are gotten through with in ten or fifteen minutes. If the

performer is particularly famous, as much as twenty
minutes may be allotted to him; but rarely more than
that.

If it is fifteen minutes, the athlete has to get through
a number of difficult and spectacular feats in that length
of time. An ordinary physical-culturist sitting in the
audience and noting the power required to do the different stunts, will wonder how in the world even the strongest man can do such an act, not just once, but a dozen
times every week.

The secret is, that the performer has carefully arranged his stunts in such order that a hard feat will be
sandwiched in between two comparatively easy ones.
And always the "big feature"—the feat which requires a
terrific output of strength and energy comes right at the
end of the act. That happens to be the correct thing to do
from the theatrical standpoint, since an act should always be arranged as to "work the audience up" to a
grand finale. But the athlete—the "Strong Man"—*has*
to do it that way; for if he did his hardest stuff at the
opening of the act, he would be very apt to do the following feats in a ragged, or sloppy manner. In order
to "put over" the impression of great strength the performer must do the hardest feats as though they were
child's play to him.

When I said that the performer alternated hard stunts
with easy ones, I meant *easy for him;* for it is but rarely
that an ordinary man, even if he is a "husky," can do
even *one* of the easiest feats in the "Strong Man's" act.
Actually some of those men are so strong that they will
rest up while doing feats that are far and away beyond
the power of the average man.

To illustrate: How many of you who read these lines
can "muscle-out" a 50-pound dumb-bell in each hand?

HENRY STEINBORN
A great lifter whose speed has enabled him to create records in snatch lifts.

Probably not more than one out of every hundred of
you. There is a "Strong Man" who does it in his act as
a "stall." Near the finish of his act he has a not very
showy, but particularly difficult act, which tires him for
a moment. Everything is set for the big finish and he
accordingly walks over and makes a bluff; tries the big
stunt and purposely fails. Then he looks around in apparent embarrassment, and happens to spy a pair of
fifty-pounders. He picks them up one in each hand,
curls them, puts them up a couple of times, and then
finally "muscles them out."

All the while he is actually smiling. And that smile
brings down the house; for every man in the audience
knows how hard it is to "muscle-out" a pair of fifties,
and is vastly impressed at seeing the stunt done with
such nonchalant ease. And while bowing in acknowledg-
ment of the applause, the performer grabs off another
thirty seconds to rest. Then feeling fresh again, he will
do the big final stunt successfully, and will walk off the
stage only to come back and take several curtain calls.

A "great showman!" you will say. I grant you all
that. But can you imagine a man so strong that a little
drill with a pair of fifties affords him not work but a
rest?

Like most other professionals, that man, when on the
road takes no exercise except what he gets in performing
his act twice a day. Why should he? Before he got on
the stage he spent months, and maybe years, in building
up his muscles, and developing his strength; and once
having gotten that strength he has no trouble in keeping
it. If he was so unwise as to do heavy exercise "on the
side," while filling an engagement, he would just be
using up the energy needed in his act; and I can assure
you that thirty minutes a day of "strength-stuff" is no

weakling's task; even if it is split up into an afternoon and evening act of fifteen minutes each.

How does all that apply to you, who have not the least desire or intention to go on the stage, or to earn your living by the strength of your muscles? The connection is that unless you were interested in great strength you would not be reading this book; and all I have been doing is to try and show you how even the strongest men train so as to avoid the *over-exercising* that prevents the building up of an energy-reserve.

Let us assume that, although you are of average size and strength, you have become seized with the ambition to become *very* strong. It may be that you feel you need the strength so as to be able to excel in your favorite sport; or it may be that you place a high value on strength for its own sake; and think it would be a glorious thing to be two or three times as strong as any of your friends.

Or perhaps you have been fascinated by the magnificent personal appearance of some celebrated "Strong Man" and have figured out that if you can get strength like his you will get a shape and development like his.

Never make the mistake of thinking that you can get strong by learning to repeat a heavy exercise, as often as you can do a light exercise of similar character. Don't figure that since you can take a 10-pound dumb-bell in your right hand and put it up 100 times, that you will be ten times as strong if you can only learn to do the same thing with a 100-pound dumb-bell. If you have already figured that way, don't try to actually *do* it.

To put up the light bell 100 times takes so little strength and energy that almost anyone can do it without becoming noticeably tired. To put up a 100-pound bell takes a great deal of strength and energy, even if you make but a few repetitions; and if you devoted all your time to making as many repetitions as possible, your muscles would get bigger but your energy would fade. Didn't you ever notice that a man after doing some particularly heavy stunt, will say, "I tell you, boys, *that takes it out of you.*" By "it" he means energy.

The cardinal rule is that the heavier the exercise the fewer times it need be repeated. This applies equally whether you are using iron weights, rubber or steel springs, or the weight of your own body. As we have already seen, to "squat" (or do the "deep knee-bend") is so easy that it soon becomes just a matter of endurance. So don't assume that because it is so darn easy to squat fifty times on both legs, it would be the proper caper to learn to make fifty squats on *one* leg. The two stunts take an entirely different kind of strength. Why, I know dozens of young fellows who can squat *one hundred times* using both legs, who have not the strength to squat even once using the strength of only one leg.

I could go on and give you similar examples of exercises for every part of your body, but these two ought to be sufficient. Work this way: As soon as an exercise becomes very easy for you, make it harder; not by increasing the number of repetitions, but by adding to the resistance the muscles have to overcome. Don't *force* yourself to repeat the heavier exercises as often as you did the lighter one, and when the heavier work becomes easy, why, make it still heavier, *and reduce the counts accordingly.*

It is possible to work that scheme on every part of the body, and you can do it either by sticking to the same set of exercises and adding progressively to the resistance; or by substituting different, but more difficult, exercises for easy ones.

After you have so practiced for a few months, you will find that instead of having to do, say, twelve exercises, each one hundred times, you do each exercise but five times each. So as an expert you do only sixty repetitions altogether; and while they make you use far more strength, they require the expenditure of far less energy. Furthermore, the strength-exercises produce an entirely different kind of muscle. Repeated strength-exercises create the maximum of size, and bring out the full beauty of outline; while the lighter exercises only produce muscles of moderate size, which have but little strength and less shape.

Now to help you guard against the second common mistake. Don't *rush* through your strength exercises. Don't jump right from one exercise to the next. Give yourself plenty of chance to rest. You should allow almost as much time to do a dozen strength-exercises, each a few times, as it took to perform the lighter exercises ten times as often. Rush your heavy work and you will finish up "all in." Take your time and you will "finish strong" with your pulse and respiration only slightly above normal, without profuse perspiration, and with a great feeling of strength and energy.

If possible, arrange the exercises on the professional's plan, spacing out the harder ones with easier ones in between.

There is no magic in exercising a particular number of minutes. Even if you have been assured that "thirty minutes a day" is the correct program, that does not mean that you will kill yourself if you exercise thirty-one minutes, or that you will fail to get results if you work for only twenty-nine. Always gauge the amount of work by the way you feel. Your work-out may call for fifteen exercises, but if you feel unusually tired by the time you have finished the twelfth, quit at once and call it a day. It is better to let one or two sets of muscles go without their regular work than to make an overdraft on your energy bank.

On the other hand, on days when you feel particularly fit, there is no harm in doing a little extra work; although instead of making the exercises harder or longer, it is better to employ that extra energy in making a couple of tests to see how strong you are getting to be.

Beware of rigid schedules. It would be exceedingly pleasant if you could go on forever gaining at the same rate of speed, but nature simply won't work that way. Don't insist that your muscles *must* be just so big on January first and just so much bigger on February first. That also goes for strength. Don't believe for one minute that you *must* be able to lift or pull so many pounds one week and so many more the next. Do your exercises as regularly as you can, and with the best of your ability, and strength and development are bound to come.

Now if you are one of those fellows who can devote only a little time each morning or evening to the pursuit of strength, while in the early stages—while the exercises are still easy—you can go through the whole lot, even if you have only thirty minutes to spare for practice. But when the exercises get harder, you will have to reduce their number if you are going to adhere to the progressive principle. This can be done in different ways—by dividing the exercises into groups. You might do all your arm, shoulder and upper-back exercises one day; all the leg and lower-back work the second day; and the chest, abdominal and side-exercises on the third day. It would seem better to mix up the exercises so that while you did only four or five exercises each day, one of them would be for your arms, another for your legs, and so on.

Under this plan you can make good progress, although you won't gain as rapidly as does the other fellow who gives up two hours to strength culture on three or four evenings of the week, and who works all his muscles at each exercise session.

Even if you are working this way, and do but little actual work every day, you may be actually in action only eight minutes out of the thirty. You must never *force* yourself to exercise every morning or night whether you feel like it or not. And whichever plan you are working on, never hesitate to "lay off" a few days if for two or three days in succession the exercises have seemed more like a laborious nuisance than an exhilarating pastime.

CHAPTER XII.

Building Strength

IF it is hard for the average citizen to realize the prodigious powers of a really strong man, it is still harder for him to understand where that power comes from.

Take, for example, when the late Louis Cyr, as a young man, actually pushed a loaded freight-car, single-handed, for a few yards up a slight grade. Tell that to the average man and he will at once say "Wow! Why, it would take a dozen ordinary men to do that"; and so he comes to the conclusion that the mighty Louis had the strength of twelve, which sounds just like the marvelous stories about the old-time heroes. The explanation is, that freight-cars were smaller thirty years ago, and that Cyr knew just how to apply his strength. At that it would have taken about four ordinary strong workmen to do any of Cyr's most famous stunts. How much can the ordinary workman "muscle out?" About 35 pounds. Cyr muscled-out 135 pounds. How much can the ordinary workman lift off the ground if he leans over and picks up the object with his hands? 300, 350 or in some cases 400 pounds. Cyr lifted around 1800 in that style. Perhaps Cyr is no fair basis for comparison, for he inherited tremendous strength, and added to that strength by practice and training, and no one, born on this side of the ocean in the last hundred years, has been able to do the things that Cyr did.

It must be remembered that Cyr, when in condition, weighed over 300 pounds himself and that he had the body of a giant, even if he was less than six feet tall. Some of our best known "Strong Men" are by no means gigantic. The bigger ones average around five feet ten inches in height and weigh anywhere from 185 to 225 pounds—all bone and muscle. No heavier, you see, than many boxers, and not as heavy as lots of those big beefy wrestlers.

There are quite a group of "Strong Men" who stand 5 feet 4, or 5 feet 6 inches and who weigh from 140 to 165 pounds. Add to that the fact that the vast majority of *modern* "Strong Men" are "self-made" and you will see that there is a chance for *anyone* to become strong, no matter what handicap nature has imposed in the way of lack of height, small bones or a slender frame. When you think of the diminutive Oscar Matthes at one end of the scale, and the gigantic Cyr at the other, and all the others of various heights, weights, and shapes in between these two, it should convince you that *you* have a chance. You probably never could get as big and strong as Cyr; in fact you would not want his clumsy build, but you can do as much for yourself as Mr. Matthes did; *if* you can equal his interest and persistence.

The general public knows little about strength, either how to get it or how to use it. Furthermore the dear public is a rotten judge of strength.

The average boy of eighteen or nineteen will judge all "Strong Men" and strength-records by the feats of his favorite hero in fiction—perhaps after the hero of some widely-read books, who performs feats that no human being ever did or could do. If he has ever seen a real "Strong Man" in the flesh, it has been at the circus or across the footlights. As the stunts of his fiction hero have enlarged his bump of credulity he is prepared to believe the actual "Strong Man" can do anything; which makes it easy for the very, *very* few fakers in the business to earn a false reputation for superhuman strength.

Why, I have had men come and ask me if *I* could lift

2000 pounds with my teeth; and when I assured them that I could lift only a small fraction of a ton in that way, they would say, "Oh, then I guess you are not as strong as So-and-So. He says *he* can do it."

Contrasted to that, there are the confirmed skeptics who hold that *all* feats of strength are accomplished through trickery, and that no one man is very much stronger than others; and that is unfair to the dozens of "Strong Men" who give exhibitions of great muscular strength, and to the hundreds of amateurs who *could* give similar exhibitions if they wished to.

It is surprising how many there are who think that because they have never seen anyone handle a dumb-bell heavier than 50 pounds, then to put up 100 pounds is as much as *anyone* can do.

Now if such a man asked any professional, or any *fairly* good amateur, "Can you put up 100 pounds with one hand?" the athlete would have regarded him as a curiosity, and would have answered, "Of course I can." And if the doubter demanded proof, the "Strong Man" would take a "hundred-pounder," and after he swung it to the shoulder, "put it up" not once, but half a dozen times. And all the time he would think his visitor was "kidding him," for to ask a "Strong Man" whether he can manage 100 pounds in an overhead lift, is something like asking a "ten-second man" whether he really can run 100 yards in 15 seconds. Having seen it done, the visitor insists on seeing the bell weighed. Being finally convinced, he then says, "Did you ever see a man lift 500 pounds off the ground?" To forestall any further questions the athlete gets together a bunch of weights, and using the "hand-and-thigh" style, lifts the mass an inch from the ground. Then he insists that the visitor weigh the stuff. So the poor chap has to lug all the different weights to the scale and when the reading shows not 500 but *1000 pounds,* he can scarcely believe his eyes. But before he does he has one more request, which is, "Would you mind letting me feel your arm." So the very much bored athlete obliges by flexing his sixteen-inch biceps, and offering it for inspection.

Like as not the next time strength happens to come into the conversation, that particular visitor will come out with, "Say, not long ago I saw a fellow lift 1000 pounds off the floor. Gee! You ought to see the arm on him."

To the uninitiated, the arm is the only thing that counts. They fail to note the interlocking chain of superb muscles, which give bodily strength; nor do they ever take into account the great *internal driving force* which the true "Strong Man" possesses.

Let us take the last story as a lesson, and see if I can show you what the visitor should have seen, and could have learned from his interview with the "Strong Man." If he had been wise he would have asked to inspect not the arm alone, but the shoulder also. It takes more than just a strong arm to "put up" a 100-pound dumb-bell; just as it takes more than a strong arm to do a "one-arm chin."

At first thought, all that seems necessary is that the arm be straightened; whereas in addition to that the whole arm has to be thrust upward. The muscles which straighten the arm are the triceps, which are on the back of the upper arm opposite the biceps (which bends the arm). If, when standing with the weight at the shoulder, you flexed only the triceps muscle, the arm would be straightened *downwards.* Since the weight has to travel upwards, the elbow must be lifted away from the body

and upwards, until it is on a level with the top of the
head.

This lifting of the arm is accomplished not by the
triceps, but by the big deltoid muscle; which is like a
triangle with its broad base fastened to the bones of the
shoulder, and its apex or point, fastened half-way down
the bone of the upper arm.

At the start of the "push-up," most of the work is
done by the deltoid, and the smaller part by the triceps.
In the latter half of the lift, when the arm is coming to
full stretch aloft, the triceps takes on the major part of
the work. Therefore, an examination would have dis-
closed that the athlete had, covering the point of his
shoulder, a grandly developed deltoid muscle which
would have impressed an expert even more than the
wonderful development of the upper arm itself.

After the athlete had lifted the thousand pounds from
the floor, the visitor could have learned more if he had
inspected the muscles of the upper back, the forearms
and the thighs, than he could by feeling the upper arm.
For in the "hand-and-thigh" style which the lifter employed, the raising of the weight is accomplished by a
powerful straightening of the legs and a strong upward
shrug of the shoulders. If the lifter happened to be in
exhibition costume, his visitor would hardly have failed
to see that he had unusually large and shapely thighs,
particularly at their upper parts where they are joined
to the hips. But he might not have noticed that just as
the weight left the floor, two immense masses of muscle
appeared on the top of the athlete's back, just below the
base of the neck.

To the novice it appears as though all one had to do
would be to stand erect and lift the weight by bending
the arms, so that the elbows moved outward and upward.

In actuality the hands are moved upward an inch or so by lifting, or shrugging, the *shoulders*. The arms are scarcely bent at the elbows, but nevertheless there is a great pull on the arm muscles. By starting with the legs only slightly bent, and then straightening them, the athlete has elevated the whole body, and so long as he can keep his body upright and his shoulder muscle taut, the weight *has* to come up. If he had stood upright and tried to lift the weight just by bending his arms, all he could have raised would be two or three hundred pounds; whereas by employing the bigger and more powerful muscles of his thighs and shoulders, he can lift four or five times as much.

Since this is a stunt of "general strength"—one which required many muscles to work in unison—I am going to improve the occasion by still further analyzing the action of the muscles used.

If you could see a photograph of an athlete lifting one thousand pounds in this manner, you would notice muscles sticking out all over him, and perhaps the most evident *would* be the big arm muscles; and you might conclude that I was all wrong when I said that the arms had but a small part of the actual lifting.

The forearm muscles naturally stand out in cords and bands, for it takes great gripping power to keep the fingers clenched when 1000 pounds is lifted. The upper-arm muscles stand out, not under lifting strain, but the *holding* strain. Remember that 500 pounds is hung from the end of each arm, and that weight is sufficient to pull the bone of the forearm loose from the bone of the upper arm bone; *and would do so* unless the strongly flexed muscles, and the rigid tendons held the joint together.

The muscles along the full length of the spine also stand out prominently, not because they do much of the lifting, but because they have to keep the body upright. The muscles which stand out most prominently of all are the ones which are doing the actual lifting; namely, the thighs and shoulder-muscles.

Let's do some more analysis, this time studying the "dip" on the parallel-bars. A strength-seeker wishes to develop the triceps muscles, which straighten the arms, and is told all that is necessary is to practice "dipping" on the parallels. The idea being that since the triceps straighten the arms, and as in dipping the body is lifted *by* straightening the arms, the performance of the act will develop the muscles used. Which is perfectly true, so far as it goes. "Dipping" is one of the grandest tri-ceps-developers, although while it adds bulk and strength to most of the triceps muscle, it leaves a smaller part in a partly developed state.

My point is that "dipping" develops other muscles even more than it develops the triceps. In doing the feat, first you mount the bars, one hand on each bar, arms unbent, and body straight up and down. All your weight is supported on your hands. Now you bend the arms at the elbows and allow your body to sink verti-cally downward between the bars. This brings your arm-pits down close to your hands, and makes your elbows stick upwards and backwards. This position stretches the breast muscles; in fact, stretches them so violently that for a man who has thin, weak breast muscles the position is actually painful.

The next thing to do is to raise from the dip; to push yourself up again. To effect this, you push against the bars with your hands just as hard as you can. But in order to get back to the first position the elbows have to be brought close to the sides of the body. That is done not by the action of the triceps, but principally by the

breast-muscles. As in the case of the deltoids the pectorals are roughly triangular in shape, with their bases
attached, or anchored to, each side of the breast-bone,
and their points to the upper arm-bones. (They have
other anchorages on the collar-bone and ribs.)

The pectorals were stretched as the body was "dipped"
or lowered. The upward motion is started by their power.
As they contract they shorten and pull the upper arm
even closer to the body. *After* the body is half-way up,
the work of lifting is further taken over by the triceps.
That is a brief and sketchy description, which leaves out
a lot; because there are other body-muscles which help
the pectorals; and the triceps really work throughout
the entire time the body is being lifted. At that this
little exposition may serve to show you how in some cases
the body-muscles do most of the work in what appears
to be a feat of arm-strength.

I have spent considerable time in showing people how
to get strength and development by using chest-expand-
ers; a device consisting of two handles connected by steel
springs, or rubber-cables. If a pupil asked me to give
him an exercise that would develop only the triceps, I
would have to tell him to proceed in this manner. To
hold the expander loosely across his chest; hold the upper
arms out horizontally to the sides so that the elbows
pointed straight out; and then to stretch the expander by
straightening the arms. Since the upper arms are held
still, the cables are stretched by moving the forearms
only; and practically all the work would be done by the
triceps, which by their contraction would bring the forearms into line with the upper arms. But that would be
a particularly poor exercise, for it would make the triceps work separately, instead of in conjunction with
other muscles. So I prefer to hold the expander across

the chest with the elbows close to the body, and the hands near the shoulders; and then to stretch the cables by pushing the hands out straight to the sides, and extending the arms as I straighten them. For that develops not only the triceps, but all the shoulder and upper-body muscles, which move the arm away from the body; the muscles you would use in "putting the shot," or in striking a hard blow with your fist.

Let us consider a feat of strength which involves the use of the arm-muscles and of the body-muscles which *control* the arms. As for example, the gymnastic stunt known as "The Cross." This is performed on a pair of swinging-rings. The whole weight of the body is on the hands. The arms are stretched out to either side and the body hangs almost upright. So the body forms the upright bar of the cross, and the arms which are rigidly straight, form the cross-bar.

This is really a terrific feat of strength, which brings into play almost every muscle from the neck to the waist, and from hands to shoulders.

To help you realize the strength required, let us suppose that a man weighing, say 150 pounds, would muscle out a 75-pound weight in each hand. Each bell would be half his own weight, and only a very strong man could hold the bells at arm-length. All his energy would be concentrated in keeping the two dumb-bells at the level of his shoulders; which would mean a violent contraction of the triceps muscles and a still more violent effort on the part of the shoulder-muscles; and only particularly big and strong muscles could withstand the strain.

When a gymnast does "The Cross," his problem is just the opposite; for his great effort is to keep his *body* from falling. So he presses against the rings with the palms of his hands, and presses so strongly that all the muscles on his arms and body stand out like steel bands. You see, his upper arms simply *must* be kept at right-angles to this body. The arms themselves have no power to maintain the position, and so that power is furnished by a pair of big muscles called the latissimi, whose broad bases are anchored to the various bones of the lower back and whose points are attached to the upper-arm bones. When these muscles contract they pull, or keep, the arms close to the body; or draw them past the body.

When doing "The Cross" these muscles hold the body up—or keep the arms level—whichever way you choose to put it. While the latissimi are working harder than any others, all the muscles are helping. We have seen that the breast-muscles and the shoulder-muscles also are anchored on the body, and attached to the arm-bones. So they have to contract and help keep the arms and body at right-angles to each other. The muscles of the upper arms and forearms flex themselves so as to keep the arms from bending at the elbow; a thing which requires a balance of forces and therefore application of power from both sides of the joint. The muscles of the upper arm itself cross the shoulder-joint and fasten to the body; and they help out. Therefore "The Cross" can be performed only by an athlete who is thoroughly and evenly developed, and who is particularly well-knit. A lack of size (and consequently of power) in any one set of muscles, would make it impossible for him to do "The Cross."

One step further: This time a stunt that employs still more muscles. There is a feat known as "making a flag" of yourself. The gymnast stands alongside of a vertical pole; grasps it with one hand at the level of his hips, and with the other hand as high as he can comfortably reach; then he lifts his feet from the ground and stretches his legs and body out horizontally. The arms are almost but not quite straight. The body and legs form the flag blown out straight by the wind, and the arms are the ropes which fasten it to the flag-pole. Gymnasts take pride in doing this stunt "stylishly." They get the body and legs in one straight line, keep the legs pressed together, and "point their toes." What is more they hold the position for a couple of seconds without a perceptible quiver. If you have followed any line of argument in the other cases, you should be able to figure out for yourselves how "doing the flag" requires strong muscles on the arms, shoulders, breast, back—particularly on the sides—and in a lesser degree on the hips, and even the thighs.

I could go on and on; for this kind of thing is one of my greatest interests. If I had the space I would analyze all sorts of strength-feats and show you how the muscles work. Earlier in the book I had to do it, to prove the combination of back and leg strength that was necessary to lie with head on one chair, feet on another, while supporting a great weight on the center of the body.

All the time I have been working in the hope of making you realize that great strength necessitates an all-round symmetrical development; that the whole body has to be considered *as a unit*, and not as a lot of unrelated parts; and that a "Strong Man" must have great bodily strength instead of just local strength. There is a vast difference between a strong *man* and a man with strong *arms*.

In your case—*you*, the strength-seeker—it is my hope that you work on the lines I have suggested. Instead of working entirely for a strength of sinew, or just for large puffy muscles, why not plan your work so as to increase your bodily strength and build up your internal energy while covering your body with muscles which are at once of large size, great strength and high quality? That kind of muscle *always* is shapely and clean-cut. With such muscles your body will be capable of lightning-like agility, or of tremendous power slowly applied.

Now for some additional hints about muscles. The common belief is that a "Strong Man's" muscles are of necessity "as hard as iron." That even when at rest and utterly relaxed his muscles are so solidly made that you cannot squeeze them out of shape. Also, that even when not in action, his muscles stand out in knots and ridges; that they are stiff and unyielding, and therefore slow to respond to the commands of the will. If there is one thing noticeable about the very strong, it is their extreme smoothness of outline. Of course, when the muscles are working they stand out in ridges or lumps, and if a professional does "muscle posing" he *deliberately* makes his muscles stand out in high relief. (And so do you when you hump up your biceps to impress a friend with your arm-development.)

If you were to watch a professional at his practice, you would notice that when he was resting, his muscles, instead of being lumped-up, would be as smooth as your own. In fact very much smoother. For *your* muscles are probably so thin that your elbows and knees are knobby. Your collar-bone and shoulder-blades protrude, so that what muscles you have, have no seeming relation to each other and are widely-spaced. Whereas, the "Strong Man" having *every* muscle developed, has long sweeping curves. His body muscles are like low-lying hills, melting into each other; and his arms and legs are far rounder than yours.

His arms are joined to his body in such a way that in certain positions the muscles seem to run in one unbroken sweep from his elbow all the way to the base of the neck, or to the breast-bone. As for collar-bones and shoulder-blades, you know he has them, but they never make themselves unpleasantly apparent. His great thighs merge right into his hips. If he happens to be half reclining on a couch, his body at the waist-line looks as round, and almost as smooth as, say, a telegraph-pole. If he starts to sit up, then for an instant you get a glimpse of a flow of muscular ridges across the front of the abdominal muscles. The abdominal muscles got busy in the act of raising the body to a sitting position. He stands squarely on both feet and his legs have beautiful smooth contours like those on the limbs of a great dancer. He takes a step forward and instantly you see the play of the great muscles on the thigh, while at the finish of each stride a great mass of muscle appears in the back of the calf.

Strong muscles have to have a certain firmness, for any flabbiness is a sign of poor condition. They should not be soft, and neither should they be *hard* to the touch.

For the life of me, I cannot understand the cause of this idea that a muscle must always be hard in order to be strong. Often you hear it said that a swimmer's muscles are the ideal type—long and smooth, and soft and shapely. They are smooth because of an extra layer of fat between the muscles and the skin. Nature's protection against chilling. (A man who swims a great deal gets that fat-layer just as naturally as a horse grows his winter coat of hair.)

If you see a picture of a group of swimmers, more likely than not they will be shown seated on the sloping bank of a stream; and almost invariably they sit with their knees drawn up, and their hands clasped over their shins. Since they wear extremely abbreviated garments,

BOBBY PANDOUR
It is evident when one beholds a development such as this
that strength is extraordinary.

you can easily see the thighs. If you are a close observer you will note that in this position the thigh is flat along the top, and has a great curve along its under side, from the inner hinge of the knee to where it reaches the hip. Therefore, the thigh muscle is sagging of its own weight, which is possible only when the muscle is flexible and relaxed. Photograph them standing on their feet and most of the muscle would show on the front of the thighs. I have often seen a bunch of "Strong Men" sitting in the position described, and have remarked that their thigh-muscles sag just as much, and just in the same way as do a swimmer's thigh-muscles.

Get a man with a very big and powerful arm to point at something. As he stretches out his arm and keeps it there, the outline of the upper arm will change. Most of the mass of muscle between his elbow and shoulder will seem to be below the bone. Again the muscles are sagging slightly of their own weight. But they must not sag too far, for instantly the "lines" of the arms, instead of being curves of beauty, become too pronounced and become "ugly." (I make no apology for using the word "beautiful." The curves of the "Strong Man's" arms *are* beautiful, while the curves of a fat man's arm are repugnant.)

There is nothing unnatural or dangerous about a muscle being iron-hard *when in action*. Stand on your tiptoes, high as you can! Reach down and place your hand on the calf of your leg. Wow! Hard as iron, isn't it? Didn't know you had such a muscle, did you? Next, sit on a table so that your feet won't touch the floor. *Now* feel the muscles of the calf. Utterly relaxed and soft. That is all there is to it.

It is possible for a man to exercise every day in the year, and for years on end, without ever getting strong;

that is, what *I* call strong. In all that time he has been on the wrong track, and has done none of the things that create strength.

He has spent enough time at his exercise to have become a wonder. What he lacked was knowledge. His principal error has been to develop the muscles singly instead of in groups. His second, that almost all his exercises have been aimed at developing a few parts of his body; probably his biceps, the front of his thighs and his abdominal muscles. Thirdly, he has never realized that muscles have to be nourished, as well as exercised. Lastly, because he has no idea of creating reserve-energy.

Many is the time some young chap has said to me, 'Mr. Liederman, why is it that I cannot get stronger? I exercise an hour at a time and I never miss a day. And I always work until my muscles are thoroughly tired." If you have read the preceding chapters *you* know why he made no progress.

After all the great trouble is that beginners will rarely take the trouble to become acquainted with the names and functions of their own muscles. Some of them know only the "biceps" by name; and the vast majority cannot —to save their lives—name a dozen separate muscles and tell what they do. Consequently, it is no wonder that they have a partial or an uneven development. If one doesn't know how the different muscles work, how can one devise exercises to develop those muscles?

One time I took a friend of mine to witness the training of a "Strong Man." It was necessary for the athlete to shift a big "pyramid weight," so that we could find a seat. And he shifted it a foot to one side with an almost imperceptible movement. Said my friend, "Say! How much does that weigh?" He was told "350 pounds," and then to me, "But, Earle, he did not lean over or seem to

use his arm very much. How did he do it?" I replied,
"After he took hold with his hand he shrugged his right
shoulder so as to lift the weight a hair's breadth, and then
he slid it along the bench. It isn't hard to do if you have
strong trapezius muscles." Further conversation proved
that my friend had never heard of those muscles; had no
idea where they were located; or what they did. So I
had the athlete stand with his back towards us, and first
shrug the shoulders, and then press the shoulder-blades
towards each other; with the result that the trapezius
stood out in masses. And then I had to still further explain that, "No, those muscles were not unnatural."
"That *everybody* had them, but usually in an undeveloped state." "That *he* could develop his trapezius muscles by doing certain things, and so on and so on."

He was not a bit worse than many others. I have seen
earnest workers spend ten minutes working their upper-
arm muscles and not ten seconds at their deltoids. Men
who would do unending exercises for the muscles on the
front of the thighs, and not one exercise for the muscles
on the rear part of the thighs. Others who spent a lot of
trouble in building up their abdominal muscles (stomach
muscles, they called them), and never did one thing to
strengthen the vastly important muscles that compose
the buttocks.

Is it any wonder that strength is a thing that always
eludes them? When they do not even know that throwing and striking power does not come from big arm-
muscles, but from the power of the body-muscles that
move the arm! Or that the legs can exert much more
power if the hip-muscles are properly developed.

Unless a man knows something about the *inter-*
dependence (not *in*dependence) of the muscles, he is little
likely ever to get a symmetrically built body. It is my

experience that symmetry is most easily acquired by means of general exercises, which use the muscles in groups, than by purely local exercises.

There is still another way in which ignorance of anatomy will handicap the man who is strong for a maximum development. In speaking of the upper arm, I mentioned only two muscles: the biceps which bends the arm, and the triceps, which straightens it. There are more muscles than that in the upper arm—smaller and less important ones—but you should know something about them, and occasionally try something else than the customary arm-exercise, so as to give development to these minor muscles.

The same thing applies to other parts of the body, particularly to the legs. Some of the larger muscles are superficial, near the skin, and others are "deep-seated," that is, close to the bone, and under the other muscles. Sometimes a man will do an exercise that develops only the big superficial muscles, and fails to do other exercises which affect the under-muscles. As a result, the limb never attains its full size. If the deep-seated muscles are developed *they push the superficial muscles outward*, and thus add considerably to the size of the limb, and also improve its contours.

The "road to strength" is not a particularly easy one to travel. It is something like the edge of a saw-blade. You go on nicely for a while, and then for a while you seem to stand still. Then you make another gain, followed by another period in which you seem to make no progress. The great thing is not to quit the first time you get stuck; but to see whether all that is necessary is to *give nature a chance to catch up.*

Above all, and this is the last piece of advice, don't forget to build up your energy-reserve by the right kind of food, plenty of sleep and the avoidance of over-exertion.

It is possible to buy the chassis, say, of a Mack truck, and put a Ford engine in it; but although the chassis is massive enough to bear 5 tons of goods, the blamed engine won't pull them. You could get more mere work done by mounting a powerful engine on a light chassis, especially on an uphill road. But why not get all the results you can; strength of chassis plus great engine-power? Make your body into a sort of Locomobile, or Rolls Royce.

The Science of Wrestling

and

The Art of Jiu Jitsu

By EARLE LIEDERMAN

THE most elaborate instructions in wrestling ever produced; highly illustrated from life, together with a most detailed course in Jiu Jitsu—the most dangerous art of self-defense ever practiced by mankind. Each and every hold, if fully executed, means a broken bone or fatal results. With such knowledge in your possession you need never fear attack, whether your opponent be armed or unarmed. The Jiu Jitsu education is so complete and so simply described that this alone is worth far more than the price asked for the entire book.

The course in wrestling is complete to the minutest detail. No doubt you have frequently wondered how a professional wrestler has thrown a man twice his size, or how some of our former lightweight champions have succeeded in throwing practically any man, no matter what his size or weight might be. These trick holds are simple enough if you could only learn them, but few know them and the professionals do not care to disclose them to the public.

THE SECRET TOLD

Earle Liederman has been severely criticized by numerous wrestlers for revealing these secrets, but he ignored unjust criticism. He determined to present this knowledge to his pupils and readers.

Suppose this very night some thug should attack you? Suppose a man many pounds heavier than you and well armed should attempt to hold you up, what would you not give to know how to immediately place him at your mercy? You will find just such information as this in "The Science of Wrestling."

This book is not for sale at book-stores or news-stands. It cannot be bought anywhere in the world except from Earle Liederman, for it is a private edition.

This book will prove a revelation to you. You will marvel at it. It contains nearly two hundred full-page photographs, the size of each page being 6 x 9 inches. It is handsomely bound in leatheroid cover, embossed in blue and gold, and is worthy of a prominent place in anyone's library collection.

PRICE, POSTPAID, $3.00

Muscle Building

By Earle Liederman

HOW would you like to have Earle Liederman visit your home? Would you like to have him sit right there alongside of you and answer all those thousands of questions about muscle building? Well, here is your chance to have him do everything but that.

Earle Liederman has kept a record of all those thousands of questions his pupils and friends have asked him, and now answers them in one of his best works—"MUSCLE BUILDING"—just as though you were sitting there face to face.

Here it is: An intensely interesting, thrilling, fascinating masterpiece that will hold you spellbound until you have reached the last page. It's one of those books that just grip you and hold you right to the finish. A big, powerful book by a big, powerful man. It literally breathes the very spirit of the author. In fact, it is Earle Liederman himself in book form.

This book is an accumulation of many years of study and research. Every bit of muscle-building information contained within its covers is fundamentally sound and based on personal contact and investigation by Earle Liederman himself. It contains the most impressive collection of photographs ever assembled in book form, 224 pages of straight-from-the-shoulder muscle-building advice. There is a punch in every chapter and a lesson on every page.

❦

What Others Say:

" Highly educational, a wonderful work."

"A book with a kick by a man with a punch."

"It drives the truth home with a bang."

" Nothing like it on the market."

"Worth ten times what you ask."

"Should be in the public schools."

A volume de luxe. Handsomely bound in green leatheroid cover, embossed in gold. Nearly 100 full-page photographs of the world's strongest and best-developed men. The entire volume covers every subject pertaining to muscular development imaginable. Not a thing left unsaid. IT'S THE LAST WORD.

Price $3.00

Here's Health

By

Earle Liederman

▬▬

I N this book the author steps away from his usual emphasis on muscles and strength, and gives you straight-from-the-shoulder talks on physiology and hygiene.

This is one of the brightest and breeziest books of its kind ever written. Full of pep and shows another side of Earle Liederman's life.

You have always pictured Earle Liederman as a stern, serious man, who never laughs. Well, he does laugh, for he has a remarkable sense of humor, and you too will laugh at some of the comparisons and characters he portrays within these pages.

If you want to know how to take care of yourself—if you want to learn about the inside of your wonderful body, don't miss reading this gripping, intensely interesting book. It is not the usual dull and dry and hard-to-get-interested-in treatise on physiology, but a highly interesting and entertaining book that is as easy to read as a story—and chock full of sound common sense and helpful advice.

It covers every organ of the human anatomy—goes straight to the point about the part of each organ in the work and health of the body and shows how to keep each organ functioning at its best.

Price $1.75

▬▬

Did you know Earle Liederman once studied to become a physician? After spending over four years at this study he suddenly gave it up, because he decided he would rather help people prevent and overcome sickness and weakness by strengthening and building up their bodies in NATURAL *ways than to doctor sick people by prescribing drugs.*

DUMB-BELLS

and

BAR-BELLS

AT SPECIAL LOW PRICES

——◆—◆◆◆—◆——

For the benefit of readers of this book who desire to obtain dumb-bells and bar-bells, I shall, upon request, be pleased to quote special money-saving prices. I am able to supply standard makes of bar-bells, dumb-bells and exercisers at a lower price than any reader can obtain direct from the various manufacturers. ❡ Let it be understood, I am not in the apparatus business, but am a builder of men. But I am ready and willing to do everything I can to help the reader secure a well developed strong body—so the privilege of saving money through me on exercisers and dumb-bells is extended to my readers as a special convenience and extra service to them in getting the fullest benefits from the advice and suggestions contained in this book.

EARLE LIEDERMAN